The DAILY WORSHIP BOOK

MICHAEL HOWARD

 Press

The Daily Worship Book
Copyright © 2024 by Michael Howard, Jr.

Published by G3 Press
4979 GA-5
Douglasville, GA 30135
www.G3Min.org

Printed in the United States of America by Graphic Response, Atlanta, GA.

ISBN: 978-1-959908-23-4

CONTENTS

INTRODUCTION

When you pray, do you usually talk to God spontaneously? When you think of worship, do you tend to think of what you do with other Christians on Sunday mornings? If your answer to those questions is, "Yes," then you are a lot like me. And that means you probably recoiled when you first considered the idea of a book of written prayers. Maybe you grew uncomfortable at the suggestion of a book for daily worship because it feels a bit too much like mainline, denominational Christianity. But the reality is, using a book for daily worship and reading written prayers to God is not a habit that belongs to Anglicans and Lutherans alone. Instead, these are habits that have been used by Christians from a multitude of theological backgrounds for almost 700 years.

While the idea of a book for daily worship and prayer might be novel to the modern day evangelical, that doesn't mean it should be. In fact, we have seen a change in approach over the last few years in this area. As pastors like Patrick Morrow and W. David Stone have sought to create a version of the *Book of Common Prayer* for their fellow Baptists, resources like *The Valley of Vision*, *Piercing Heaven: Prayers of the Puritans*, *Every Moment Holy*, and Jonathan Gibson's, *Be Thou My Vision* have gained traction with many evangelicals.

Several years ago, I felt discontent with my own daily time with the Lord. I was reading my Bible and I was praying, but there were so many days where my thoughts and words seemed aimless. This was incredibly frustrating for me because as a pastor I was supposed to be modeling a healthy prayer life for the church. It was around this time that I began to use a daily guide for worship. In my case, I chose the aforementioned *Be Thou My Vision* by Jonathan Gibson. It is a brilliant daily liturgy that puts you through the paces of praise, prayer, confession, Scripture reading, catechisms, and creeds. Suddenly, I was zooming. My time with the Lord grew from a loosely structured, "hit and miss" time of prayer and Scripture reading, to a well-defined daily worship experience before the throne of God. I told a friend of mine, "I feel like I am flying through heaven and seeing the glory of Christ when I use this book in my daily worship." I meant it.

With that in mind, I began to be convicted that I wanted to share my discovery with my church. As a shepherd, I don't want to hoard quiet waters and green pastures. I want to guide our flock into them to taste the glory of God in Christ. But how could I convince them that it is a good idea to embark on this journey? After talking with our other pastors, I decided that simply putting Gibson's book in the hands of our members would not do. We needed a liturgy of our own that was designed for the people of Seaford Baptist Church.

So that is how this came about. That is how we got here. A pastor wanted a daily prayer book for his congregation. A book that would keep the church unified, pursuing Jesus together with hearts and minds being of one accord (Acts 1:14; 2:1; 2:46). And now, by God's good governing, the book has landed in your hands. But maybe you still aren't convinced. Let's tackle some frequently asked questions.

DOES GOD REALLY WANT US TO READ WRITTEN PRAYERS TO HIM?

That is a great question because the heart behind it is one that is concerned with worshiping in spirit and in truth (John 4:24). That is a good thing. And ultimately, the answer comes down to just that—the heart. God does not want us to read prayers to Him if we do not mean them. But if we pray those words from our hearts, He loves them. Christians have recited written prayers to the Lord, including the Psalms themselves, for centuries. And the benefit is only found if the one praying truly directs those words to the Lord.

WHY ARE WRITTEN PRAYERS BENEFICIAL?

Sometimes when I go to pray, I find myself struggling for traction. The issue is not with God—it is with me. Spiritually speaking, my well is dry. My prayers seem cold and distant because I am still looking into a mirror dimly (1 Cor 13:12). Written prayers help to prime the pump of my heart and get me into a Christ-centered mindset. By the time I reach the end of my time with the Lord, and I do pray to Him spontaneously, my prayers are much more honest, focused and biblical.

WHY IS THIS BOOK BETTER THAN A USUAL CHRISTIAN DEVOTIONAL BOOK?

Devotional books can be wonderful supplements to our time with Jesus. But devotional books are not concerned with a full time of daily worship for the Christian heart. They tend to be aimed at helping you glean an application point or two from the Scriptures—not a full order of daily worship.

This book is designed to take you through a full liturgy of worship each day, complete with many of the elements you might experience in a weekly worship gathering in your local church. While time in the Word of God is one of the most important features of the daily order of worship in this book, it is enriched by the reverent engagement with God that is around it.

WHAT IS THE DAILY ORDER OF WORSHIP IN THIS BOOK?

Call to Worship from the Scriptures
The Votum (*Psalm 124:8*)
Prayer of Confession
Assurance of Forgiveness from the Scriptures
Psalm
Prayer of Illumination
Daily Bible Reading
Personal Intercession
The Lord's Prayer
Doxology

HOW DID YOU COME UP WITH THE DAILY ORDER?

There were many choices for the daily order of worship that could be used in this book. In the end, I chose an order of worship based on what was used by John Calvin in churches in Geneva during the Protestant Reformation. I say it is an adjusted version because I have added in:

Call to Worship from the Scriptures
Doxology

WHERE DO THE WRITTEN PRAYERS COME FROM?

I pulled them from various sources. Each prayer will have its original author listed below it.

WHAT ARE THESE DIFFERENT ELEMENTS OF DAILY WORSHIP?

Call to Worship from the Scriptures: A selected reading that calls us to come before the Lord in worship and adoration

The Votum: This word comes from the Latin word for "vow." Typically, *Psalm 124:8* is used for this element of worship

Prayer of Confession: A selected written prayer for the purpose of confessing sin to God

Assurance of Forgiveness from the Scriptures: A selected reading that reminds us of the forgiveness we are promised as believers

Psalm: A daily Psalm for worship and reflection

Prayer of Illumination: A selected written prayer that asks God to help us understand His Word

Daily Bible Reading: This is where you read from whatever daily Bible reading plan you are using. See the next section for suggestions.

Personal Intercession: A time for spontaneous prayer, guided by four general categories

The Lord's Prayer: Jesus' prescribed model prayer for His followers from Matthew 6:9-13

Doxology: A short hymn of praise that has been sung by Christians all over the world for more than 300 years

WHAT BIBLE READING PLAN SHOULD I BE USING?

There is no shortage of Bible reading plans available to Christians these days. A quick Google search will yield plenty of results. However, for our purposes, I will suggest two:

The Booker T. Washington Plan: This is where you read one chapter of the Bible a day. It will take just over three years to read through the whole Bible at this pace.

The McCheyne Bible Reading Plan: A diverse plan that gives you readings from the Old Testament, New Testament and Psalms each day. It takes one year to complete the plan.

HOW DO I USE THE BOOK?

This is the final question and probably the most important question. However, the great news is that it has a simple answer.

Carve out 20-30 minutes a day where you are able to get alone with the Lord. We recommend you read the words of the prayers and Scriptures out loud.

Go through the entire order of worship, and engage with each portion of the daily liturgy. This will include your daily Bible reading time, as well as a time of spontaneous prayer. Depending on your Bible reading plan and how long you pray, you may need longer than 20-30 minutes.

There are 31 different liturgies in this book. That means there is always one that corresponds with each day of the month. When the month ends, flip back to the beginning of the book and start again. There are also liturgies for a handful of special days in the Appendix.

Lastly, there is no need to be a legalist. If you miss a day, just go on to the next one. You will use that missed liturgy in a future month. If there is a day where you only have time for Bible reading and you have to skip the rest of the liturgy, that is just fine. There are no hard and fast rules here. Just worship the Lord. I pray this guide will be a help as you do.

DAY 1

CALL TO WORSHIP

Exodus 15:1–2
Then Moses and the people of Israel sang this song to the LORD, saying, "I will sing to the LORD, for he has triumphed gloriously; the horse and his rider he has thrown into the sea. The LORD is my strength and my song, and he has become my salvation; this is my God, and I will praise him, my father's God, and I will exalt him.

VOTUM

Psalm 124:8
Our help is in the name of the LORD, who made heaven and earth.

CONFESSION

Almighty and most merciful Father; We have erred, and strayed from thy ways like lost sheep. We have followed too much the devices and desires of our own hearts. We have offended against thy holy laws. We have left undone those things which we ought to have done; And we have done those things which we ought not to have done; And there is no health in us. But thou, O Lord, have mercy upon us, miserable offenders. Spare thou those, O God, who confess their faults. Restore thou those who are penitent; According to thy promises declared unto mankind in Christ Jesus our Lord. And grant, O most merciful Father, for his sake; That we may hereafter live a godly, righteous, and sober life, To the glory of thy holy Name. Amen. (*The Book of Common Prayer*, 1789)

ASSURANCE OF FORGIVENESS

1 John 5:11–13
And this is the testimony, that God gave us eternal life, and this life is in his Son. Whoever has the Son has life; whoever does not have the Son of God does not have life. I write these things to you who believe in the name of the Son of God, that you may know that you have eternal life.

PSALM OF PRAISE

Psalm 100
Make a joyful noise to the LORD, all the earth!
　　Serve the LORD with gladness!
　　Come into his presence with singing!
Know that the LORD, he is God!
　　It is he who made us, and we are his;
　　we are his people, and the sheep of his pasture.
Enter his gates with thanksgiving,
　　and his courts with praise!
　　Give thanks to him; bless his name!
For the LORD is good;
　　his steadfast love endures forever,
　　and his faithfulness to all generations.

PRAYER OF ILLUMINATION

O Lord, You have given us Your Word for a light to shine upon our path. Grant us so to meditate on that Word, and to follow its teaching that we may find in it the light that shines more and more until the perfect day. Through Jesus Christ, our Lord. Amen. (Jerome, 4th century)

DAILY BIBLE READING

Use the Bible Reading Plan of your choice.

DAILY INTERCESSION

Pray for:

> Missions and Evangelism
> Local church members and needs
> Global, National and Local Leaders and Issues
> Personal Needs and Holiness

THE LORD'S PRAYER

Our Father in heaven, hallowed be Your name, Your kingdom come, Your will be done, on earth as in heaven. Give us today our daily bread. Forgive us our sins, as we forgive those who sin against us. Lead us not into temptation, but deliver us from evil. For the kingdom, the power, and the glory are Yours now and forever. Amen.

DOXOLOGY

Sing or say these words out loud:

> Praise God from whom all blessings flow;
> Praise Him all creatures here below;
> Praise Him above ye heavenly hosts;
> Praise Father, Son and Holy Ghost.
> Amen.

Day 2

CALL TO WORSHIP

Psalm 136:1–2
Give thanks to the LORD, for he is good,
    for his steadfast love endures forever.
Give thanks to the God of gods,
    for his steadfast love endures forever.

VOTUM

Psalm 124:8
Our help is in the name of the LORD, who made heaven and earth.

CONFESSION

You see me coming into your presence as if I was forced. And when I am before you, my spirit is so empty that I hardly know what to say to you–though you are my God, and there could never be anything more important than time spent with you. Even when I do speak with you, my prayer is cold and formal. What happened to the passion I once felt, the intense pursuit of you, O God? And what happened to the wonderful rest I had in you, that feeling of just being happy to be near you–and my determination to never stray from your presence? Search me, Lord, and try me. Get the root of this disease which spreads itself over my soul, and heal me. Show me my sin, Lord, that I may see its horror. Show me Jesus in such a light that I may look upon Him and love. Amen. (Philip Doddridge[1])

ASSURANCE OF FORGIVENESS

Ephesians 2:4–5
But God, being rich in mercy, because of the great love with which he loved us, even when we were dead in our trespasses, made us alive together with Christ—by grace you have been saved.

PSALM OF PRAISE

Psalm 149
Praise the LORD!
Sing to the LORD a new song,
    his praise in the assembly of the godly!
Let Israel be glad in his Maker;
    let the children of Zion rejoice in their King!
Let them praise his name with dancing,
    making melody to him with tambourine and lyre!
For the LORD takes pleasure in his people;
    he adorns the humble with salvation.
Let the godly exult in glory;
    let them sing for joy on their beds.
Let the high praises of God be in their throats
    and two-edged swords in their hands,
to execute vengeance on the nations
    and punishments on the peoples,

to bind their kings with chains
    and their nobles with fetters of iron,
to execute on them the judgment written!
    This is honor for all his godly ones.
Praise the LORD!

PRAYER OF ILLUMINATION

Living God, help us so to hear Your holy Word that we may truly understand; that, understanding, we may believe and believing, we may follow in all faithfulness and obedience, seeking Your honor and glory in all that we do; through Christ our Lord. Amen. (Ulrych Zwingli[2])

DAILY BIBLE READING

Use the Bible Reading Plan of your choice.

DAILY INTERCESSION

Pray for:

    Missions and Evangelism
    Local church members and needs
    Global, National and Local Leaders and Issues
    Personal Needs and Holiness

THE LORD'S PRAYER

Our Father in heaven, hallowed be Your name, Your kingdom come, Your will be done, on earth as in heaven. Give us today our

daily bread. Forgive us our sins, as we forgive those who sin against us. Lead us not into temptation, but deliver us from evil. For the kingdom, the power, and the glory are Yours now and forever. Amen.

DOXOLOGY

Sing or say these words out loud:

> Praise God from whom all blessings flow;
> Praise Him all creatures here below;
> Praise Him above ye heavenly hosts;
> Praise Father, Son and Holy Ghost.
> Amen.

DAY 3

CALL TO WORSHIP

Hebrews 13:15
Through him then let us continually offer up a sacrifice of praise to God, that is, the fruit of lips that acknowledge his name.

VOTUM

Psalm 124:8
Our help is in the name of the LORD, who made heaven and earth.

CONFESSION

O Lord, with heartfelt sorrow we repent and deplore our offenses. We condemn ourselves and our evil ways, with true penitence, entreating that Your grace may relieve our distress. Be pleased to have compassion on us, O most gracious God, Father of all mercies, for the sake of Your Son, Jesus Christ our Lord. And as You remove our guilt and our pollution, grant us the daily increase of the grace of Your Holy Spirit, that acknowledging from our inmost hearts our own unrighteousness, we may be touched with sorrow that shall work true repentance, and that, mortifying all sins within us, Your Spirit may produce the fruits of holiness and righteousness well-pleasing in Your sight; through Jesus Christ our Lord. Amen. (John Calvin)

17

ASSURANCE OF FORGIVENESS

Isaiah 25:9
It will be said on that day, "Behold, this is our God; we have waited for him, that he might save us. This is the LORD; we have waited for him; let us be glad and rejoice in his salvation."

PSALM OF PRAISE

Psalm 63
O God, you are my God; earnestly I seek you;
    my soul thirsts for you;
my flesh faints for you,
    as in a dry and weary land where there is no water.
So I have looked upon you in the sanctuary,
    beholding your power and glory.
Because your steadfast love is better than life,
    my lips will praise you.
So I will bless you as long as I live;
    in your name I will lift up my hands.
My soul will be satisfied as with fat and rich food,
    and my mouth will praise you with joyful lips,
when I remember you upon my bed,
    and meditate on you in the watches of the night;
for you have been my help,
    and in the shadow of your wings I will sing for joy.
My soul clings to you;
    your right hand upholds me.
But those who seek to destroy my life
    shall go down into the depths of the earth;

they shall be given over to the power of the sword;
　　they shall be a portion for jackals.
But the king shall rejoice in God;
　　all who swear by him shall exult,
　　　for the mouths of liars will be stopped.

PRAYER OF ILLUMINATION

Almighty, gracious Father, forasmuch as our whole salvation
depends upon our true understanding of Your holy Word, grant
to all of us that our hearts, being freed from worldly affairs, may
hear and apprehend Your holy Word with all diligence and faith,
that we may rightly understand Your gracious will, cherish it,
and live by it with all earnestness, to Your praise and honor;
through our Lord Jesus Christ. Amen. (Martin Bucer[3])

DAILY BIBLE READING

Use the Bible Reading Plan of your choice.

DAILY INTERCESSION

Pray for:

　　Missions and Evangelism
　　Local church members and needs
　　Global, National and Local Leaders and Issues
　　Personal Needs and Holiness

THE LORD'S PRAYER

Our Father in heaven, hallowed be Your name, Your kingdom come, Your will be done, on earth as in heaven. Give us today our daily bread. Forgive us our sins, as we forgive those who sin against us. Lead us not into temptation, but deliver us from evil. For the kingdom, the power, and the glory are Yours now and forever. Amen.

DOXOLOGY

Sing or say these words out loud:

> Praise God from whom all blessings flow;
> Praise Him all creatures here below;
> Praise Him above ye heavenly hosts;
> Praise Father, Son and Holy Ghost.
> Amen.

DAY 4

CALL TO WORSHIP

Isaiah 55:1: Come, everyone who thirsts, come to the waters; and he who has no money, come, buy and eat! Come, buy wine and milk without money and without price.

VOTUM

Psalm 124:8
Our help is in the name of the LORD, who made heaven and earth.

CONFESSION

O merciful Father, do not consider what we have done against You but what our blessed Savior has done for us. Do not consider what we have made of ourselves, but what He is making of us for You our God. O that Christ may be "wisdom and righteousness, sanctification and redemption" to every one of our souls. May His precious blood may cleanse us from all our sins, and Your Holy Spirit renew and sanctify our souls. May He crucify our flesh with its passion and lusts, and cleanse all our brothers and sisters in Christ across the earth. In Christ's name we pray, Amen. (John Wesley[4])

ASSURANCE OF FORGIVENESS

1 John 1:9
If we confess our sins, he is faithful and just to forgive us our sins
and to cleanse us from all unrighteousness.

PSALM OF PRAISE

Psalm 8
O LORD, our Lord,
> how majestic is your name in all the earth!
You have set your glory above the heavens.
> Out of the mouth of babies and infants,
you have established strength because of your foes,
> to still the enemy and the avenger.
When I look at your heavens, the work of your fingers,
> the moon and the stars, which you have set in place,
what is man that you are mindful of him,
> and the son of man that you care for him?
Yet you have made him a little lower than the heavenly beings
> and crowned him with glory and honor.
You have given him dominion over the works of your hands;
> you have put all things under his feet,
all sheep and oxen,
> and also the beasts of the field,
the birds of the heavens, and the fish of the sea,
> whatever passes along the paths of the seas.
O LORD, our Lord,
> how majestic is your name in all the earth!

PRAYER OF ILLUMINATION

Father, we believe that the whole counsel of God concerning all things necessary for Your own glory, man's salvation, faith and life, is either expressly set down or necessarily contained in the Holy Scripture. And it is complete, Lord. Nothing is to be added to it by the revelation of the Spirit or by the traditions of men. But we acknowledge our need Lord- the inward illumination of your Spirit is necessary for the saving understanding of such things as are revealed in the Word. Amen. (Adapted from *The 1689 Baptist Confession of Faith*[5])

DAILY BIBLE READING

Use the Bible Reading Plan of your choice.

DAILY INTERCESSION

Pray for:

> Missions and Evangelism
> Local church members and needs
> Global, National and Local Leaders and Issues
> Personal Needs and Holiness

THE LORD'S PRAYER

Our Father in heaven, hallowed be Your name, Your kingdom come, Your will be done, on earth as in heaven. Give us today our daily bread. Forgive us our sins, as we forgive those who sin against us. Lead us not into temptation, but deliver us from evil.

For the kingdom, the power, and the glory are Yours now and forever. Amen.

DOXOLOGY

Sing or say these words out loud:

> Praise God from whom all blessings flow;
> Praise Him all creatures here below;
> Praise Him above ye heavenly hosts;
> Praise Father, Son and Holy Ghost.
> Amen.

Day 5

CALL TO WORSHIP

Colossians 3:16
Let the word of Christ dwell in you richly, teaching and admonishing one another in all wisdom, singing psalms and hymns and spiritual songs, with thankfulness in your hearts to God.

VOTUM

Psalm 124:8
Our help is in the name of the LORD, who made heaven and earth.

CONFESSION

Narrow is the mansion of my soul. Enlarge it, so that You can enter. It lies in ruins. Repair it. I know and confess that You will find corruption there that is offensive to Your eyes. But who else shall clean it? To whom can I cry except You? Lord, scrub away my secret faults. Save Your servant from the power of the enemy. Since I believe You, I call to You, Lord, for You alone know. Haven't I given testimony of my sins to You? Haven't You forgiven the wickedness of my heart? I don't argue with Your judgment, for You are Truth. I fear my own self-deception, for my corrupt heart lies even to itself. I offer no defense against Your judgment, for if You, Lord, kept a record of sins, who could stand? (Augustine[6])

ASSURANCE OF FORGIVENESS

Psalm 32:1
Blessed is the one whose transgression is forgiven,
>   whose sin is covered.

PSALM OF PRAISE

Psalm 113
Praise the LORD!
Praise, O servants of the LORD,
>   praise the name of the LORD!
Blessed be the name of the LORD
>   from this time forth and forevermore!
From the rising of the sun to its setting,
>   the name of the LORD is to be praised!
The LORD is high above all nations,
>   and his glory above the heavens!
Who is like the LORD our God,
>   who is seated on high,
who looks far down
>   on the heavens and the earth?
He raises the poor from the dust
>   and lifts the needy from the ash heap,
to make them sit with princes,
>   with the princes of his people.
He gives the barren woman a home,
>   making her the joyous mother of children.
Praise the LORD!

PRAYER OF ILLUMINATION

I know, O Lord, and tremble to think, that three parts of the good seed fell upon bad ground. Let not my heart be like the highway. Through hardness and want of true understanding it does not receive the seed, so the evil one comes and snatches it away. Let not my heart be like the stony ground, which hears with joy for a time, but falls away as soon as persecution arises for the gospel's sake. Let not my heart by like the thorny ground, which chokes the word and makes it altogether unfruitful because of the cares of this world and the deceit of riches. Let my heart by like the good ground. Help me to hear Your word with an honest and good heart. Enable me to understand and keep it, and bring forth fruit with patience, for your glory and my everlasting benefit. Amen. (Lewis Bayly[7])

DAILY BIBLE READING

Use the Bible Reading Plan of your choice.

DAILY INTERCESSION

Pray for:

> Missions and Evangelism
> Local church members and needs
> Global, National and Local Leaders and Issues
> Personal Needs and Holiness

THE LORD'S PRAYER

Our Father in heaven, hallowed be Your name, Your kingdom come, Your will be done, on earth as in heaven. Give us today our daily bread. Forgive us our sins, as we forgive those who sin against us. Lead us not into temptation, but deliver us from evil. For the kingdom, the power, and the glory are Yours now and forever. Amen.

DOXOLOGY

Sing or say these words out loud:

> Praise God from whom all blessings flow;
> Praise Him all creatures here below;
> Praise Him above ye heavenly hosts;
> Praise Father, Son and Holy Ghost.
> Amen.

Day 6

CALL TO WORSHIP

Psalm 5:7-8
But I, through the abundance of your steadfast love,
    will enter your house.
I will bow down toward your holy temple
    in the fear of you.
Lead me, O Lord, in your righteousness
    because of my enemies;
        make your way straight before me.

VOTUM

Psalm 124:8
Our help is in the name of the Lord, who made heaven and earth.

CONFESSION

But, Lord, we have yet another burden–it is that we ourselves do not love Thee as we should, that oftentimes we grow lukewarm and chill, and doubt creeps over us, and unbelief mars our confidence, and we sin and forget our God. O Lord help us! Pardon is not enough, we want sanctification. We beseech Thee let the weeds that grow in the seed plot of our soul be cut up by the roots. We do want to serve Thee. We long that every thought we think, and word we say or write, should be all for Thee. (Charles Spurgeon[8])

ASSURANCE OF FORGIVENESS

Hebrews 10:16–17
"This is the covenant that I will make with them after those days, declares the Lord: I will put my laws on their hearts, and write them on their minds," then he adds, "I will remember their sins and their lawless deeds no more."

PSALM OF PRAISE

Psalm 150
Praise the LORD!
Praise God in his sanctuary;
    praise him in his mighty heavens!
Praise him for his mighty deeds;
    praise him according to his excellent greatness!
Praise him with trumpet sound;
    praise him with lute and harp!
Praise him with tambourine and dance;
    praise him with strings and pipe!
Praise him with sounding cymbals;
    praise him with loud clashing cymbals!
Let everything that has breath praise the LORD!
Praise the LORD!

PRAYER OF ILLUMINATION

Lord, may those whom you have already visited in your grace and illumined with the knowledge of your Word grow daily in goodness, being enriched with your spiritual blessings, that we may adore you altogether with one heart and one mouth and give honor and homage to your Christ, our Master, King, and Lawgiver. (John Calvin[9])

DAILY BIBLE READING

Use the Bible Reading Plan of your choice.

DAILY INTERCESSION

Pray for:

> Missions and Evangelism
> Local church members and needs
> Global, National and Local Leaders and Issues
> Personal Needs and Holiness

THE LORD'S PRAYER

Our Father in heaven, hallowed be Your name, Your kingdom come, Your will be done, on earth as in heaven. Give us today our daily bread. Forgive us our sins, as we forgive those who sin against us. Lead us not into temptation, but deliver us from evil. For the kingdom, the power, and the glory are Yours now and forever. Amen.

DOXOLOGY

Sing or say these words out loud:

Praise God from whom all blessings flow;
Praise Him all creatures here below;
Praise Him above ye heavenly hosts;
Praise Father, Son and Holy Ghost.
Amen.

DAY 7

CALL TO WORSHIP

Hebrews 12:28-29
Therefore let us be grateful for receiving a kingdom that cannot be shaken, and thus let us offer to God acceptable worship, with reverence and awe, for our God is a consuming fire.

VOTUM

Psalm 124:8
Our help is in the name of the LORD, who made heaven and earth.

CONFESSION

Behold, Lord, an empty vessel that needs to be filled. My Lord, fill it. I am weak in the faith; strengthen me. I am cold in love; warm me and make me fervent, that my love may go out to my neighbor. I do not have a strong and firm faith; at times I doubt and am unable to trust you altogether. O Lord, help me. Strengthen my faith and trust in you. In you I have sealed the treasure of all I have. I am poor; you are rich and came to be merciful to the poor. I am a sinner; you are upright. With me, there is an abundance of sin; in you is the fullness of righteousness. Therefore I will remain with you, of whom I can receive, but to whom I may not give. Amen. (Martin Luther[10])

ASSURANCE OF FORGIVENESS

John 3:16–17
For God so loved the world, that he gave his only Son, that whoever believes in him should not perish but have eternal life. For God did not send his Son into the world to condemn the world, but in order that the world might be saved through him.

PSALM OF PRAISE

Psalm 134
Come, bless the LORD, all you servants of the LORD,
 who stand by night in the house of the LORD!
Lift up your hands to the holy place
 and bless the LORD!
May the LORD bless you from Zion,
 he who made heaven and earth!

PRAYER OF ILLUMINATION

Holy Spirit, be in me the resident witness of my Lord, the author of my prayers, the Spirit of adoption, the seal of God, and the deposit of my inheritance. Transcribe those sacred words on my heart that by Your inspiration are recorded in Your holy word. Bring that love upon my heart that may keep it in a continual life of love. Amen. (Richard Baxter[11])

DAILY BIBLE READING

Use the Bible Reading Plan of your choice.

DAILY INTERCESSION

Pray for:

Missions and Evangelism
Local church members and needs
Global, National and Local Leaders and Issues
Personal Needs and Holiness

THE LORD'S PRAYER

Our Father in heaven, hallowed be Your name, Your kingdom come, Your will be done, on earth as in heaven. Give us today our daily bread. Forgive us our sins, as we forgive those who sin against us. Lead us not into temptation, but deliver us from evil. For the kingdom, the power, and the glory are Yours now and forever. Amen.

DOXOLOGY

Sing or say these words out loud:

Praise God from whom all blessings flow;
Praise Him all creatures here below;
Praise Him above ye heavenly hosts;
Praise Father, Son and Holy Ghost.
Amen.

DAY 8

CALL TO WORSHIP

Isaiah 6:1–3

In the year that King Uzziah died I saw the Lord sitting upon a throne, high and lifted up; and the train of his robe filled the temple. Above him stood the seraphim. Each had six wings: with two he covered his face, and with two he covered his feet, and with two he flew. And one called to another and said: "Holy, holy, holy is the LORD of hosts; the whole earth is full of his glory!"

VOTUM

Psalm 124:8

Our help is in the name of the LORD, who made heaven and earth.

CONFESSION

Have mercy on me, O God,
    according to your steadfast love;
according to your abundant mercy
    blot out my transgressions.
Wash me thoroughly from my iniquity,
    and cleanse me from my sin!
For I know my transgressions,
    and my sin is ever before me.
Against you, you only, have I sinned
    and done what is evil in your sight,

so that you may be justified in your words
and blameless in your judgment. Amen. (Psalm 51:1–4)

ASSURANCE OF FORGIVENESS

Isaiah 43:25
I, I am he who blots out your transgressions for my own sake, and
I will not remember your sins.

PSALM OF PRAISE

Psalm 95
Oh come, let us sing to the LORD;
let us make a joyful noise to the rock of our salvation!
Let us come into his presence with thanksgiving;
let us make a joyful noise to him with songs of praise!
For the LORD is a great God,
and a great King above all gods.
In his hand are the depths of the earth;
the heights of the mountains are his also.
The sea is his, for he made it,
and his hands formed the dry land.
Oh come, let us worship and bow down;
let us kneel before the LORD, our Maker!
For he is our God,
and we are the people of his pasture,
and the sheep of his hand.
Today, if you hear his voice,
do not harden your hearts,
as at Meribah, as on the day at Massah in the wilderness,

when your fathers put me to the test
and put me to the proof, though they had seen my work.
For forty years I loathed that generation
and said, "They are a people who go astray in their heart,
and they have not known my ways."
Therefore I swore in my wrath,
"They shall not enter my rest."

PRAYER OF ILLUMINATION

Lord, I am now entering into Your presence, to hear You speak from heaven to me, to receive Your rain and spiritual dew, which never return in vain, but ripen a harvest either of corn or weeds, of grace or judgment. My heart is prepared, O Lord, my heart is prepared to learn and to love any of Your words. Your law is my counselor; I will be ruled by it. It is my physician; I will be a patient under it. It is my schoolmaster; I will be obedient to it. Amen. (Edward Reynolds[12])

DAILY BIBLE READING

Use the Bible Reading Plan of your choice.

DAILY INTERCESSION

Pray for:

Missions and Evangelism
Local church members and needs

Global, National and Local Leaders and Issues
Personal Needs and Holiness

THE LORD'S PRAYER

Our Father in heaven, hallowed be Your name, Your kingdom come, Your will be done, on earth as in heaven. Give us today our daily bread. Forgive us our sins, as we forgive those who sin against us. Lead us not into temptation, but deliver us from evil. For the kingdom, the power, and the glory are Yours now and forever. Amen.

DOXOLOGY

Sing or say these words out loud:

Praise God from whom all blessings flow;
Praise Him all creatures here below;
Praise Him above ye heavenly hosts;
Praise Father, Son and Holy Ghost.
Amen.

DAY 9

CALL TO WORSHIP

Colossians 1:15–17
He is the image of the invisible God, the firstborn of all creation. For by him all things were created, in heaven and on earth, visible and invisible, whether thrones or dominions or rulers or authorities—all things were created through him and for him. And he is before all things, and in him all things hold together.

VOTUM

Psalm 124:8
Our help is in the name of the LORD, who made heaven and earth.

CONFESSION

Dearest Lord Jesus, I blush when I think of how Your glory was veiled in humiliation; and then I compare it to how often my poor fallen nature has been hurt by some imagined, trivial offense. I desire the same attitude as Yours, Jesus, when You humbled Yourself. Amen. (Robert Hawker[13])

ASSURANCE OF FORGIVENESS

Hebrews 8:12
For I will be merciful toward their iniquities, and I will remember their sins no more."

PSALM OF PRAISE

Psalm 29
Ascribe to the LORD, O heavenly beings,
  ascribe to the LORD glory and strength.
Ascribe to the LORD the glory due his name;
  worship the LORD in the splendor of holiness.
The voice of the LORD is over the waters;
  the God of glory thunders,
  the LORD, over many waters.
The voice of the LORD is powerful;
  the voice of the LORD is full of majesty.
The voice of the LORD breaks the cedars;
  the LORD breaks the cedars of Lebanon.
He makes Lebanon to skip like a calf,
  and Sirion like a young wild ox.
The voice of the LORD flashes forth flames of fire.
The voice of the LORD shakes the wilderness;
  the LORD shakes the wilderness of Kadesh.
The voice of the LORD makes the deer give birth
  and strips the forests bare,
  and in his temple all cry, "Glory!"
The LORD sits enthroned over the flood;
  the LORD sits enthroned as king forever.
May the LORD give strength to his people!
  May the LORD bless his people with peace!

PRAYER OF ILLUMINATION

Almighty God, and most merciful Father, we humbly submit ourselves, and fall down before Your Majesty, asking You from the bottom of our hearts, that this seed of Your word now sown among us, may take such deep root, that neither the burning heat of persecution cause it to wither, nor the thorny cares of this life choke it. But that, as seed sown in good ground, it may bring forth thirty, sixty, or a hundredfold, as Your heavenly wisdom has appointed. Amen. (Middelburg Liturgy[14])

DAILY BIBLE READING

Use the Bible Reading Plan of your choice.

DAILY INTERCESSION

Pray for:

> Missions and Evangelism
> Local church members and needs
> Global, National and Local Leaders and Issues
> Personal Needs and Holiness

THE LORD'S PRAYER

Our Father in heaven, hallowed be Your name, Your kingdom come, Your will be done, on earth as in heaven. Give us today our daily bread. Forgive us our sins, as we forgive those who sin against us. Lead us not into temptation, but deliver us from evil.

For the kingdom, the power, and the glory are Yours now and forever. Amen.

DOXOLOGY

Sing or say these words out loud:

> Praise God from whom all blessings flow;
> Praise Him all creatures here below;
> Praise Him above ye heavenly hosts;
> Praise Father, Son and Holy Ghost.
> Amen.

Day 10

John 4:21–24

Jesus said to her, "Woman, believe me, the hour is coming when neither on this mountain nor in Jerusalem will you worship the Father. You worship what you do not know; we worship what we know, for salvation is from the Jews. But the hour is coming, and is now here, when the true worshipers will worship the Father in spirit and truth, for the Father is seeking such people to worship him. God is spirit, and those who worship him must worship in spirit and truth."

VOTUM

Psalm 124:8

Our help is in the name of the LORD, who made heaven and earth.

CONFESSION

O Lord, I am a lost and fallen creature both by nature and by innumerable actual transgressions, which I confess before you this day. You have revealed to me and impressed on my heart my miserable state, and made manifest the remedy you provide by Christ. Amen. (William Guthrie[15])

ASSURANCE OF FORGIVENESS

Romans 8:35–39

Who shall separate us from the love of Christ? Shall tribulation, or distress, or persecution, or famine, or nakedness, or danger, or sword? As it is written, "For your sake we are being killed all the day long; we are regarded as sheep to be slaughtered." No, in all these things we are more than conquerors through him who loved us. For I am sure that neither death nor life, nor angels nor rulers, nor things present nor things to come, nor powers, nor height nor depth, nor anything else in all creation, will be able to separate us from the love of God in Christ Jesus our Lord.

PSALM OF PRAISE

Psalm 19

The heavens declare the glory of God,
    and the sky above proclaims his handiwork.
Day to day pours out speech,
    and night to night reveals knowledge.
There is no speech, nor are there words,
    whose voice is not heard.
Their voice goes out through all the earth,
    and their words to the end of the world.
In them he has set a tent for the sun,
    which comes out like a bridegroom leaving his chamber,
    and, like a strong man, runs its course with joy.
Its rising is from the end of the heavens,
    and its circuit to the end of them,
    and there is nothing hidden from its heat.

The law of the LORD is perfect,
  reviving the soul;
the testimony of the LORD is sure,
  making wise the simple;
the precepts of the LORD are right,
  rejoicing the heart;
the commandment of the LORD is pure,
  enlightening the eyes;
the fear of the LORD is clean,
  enduring forever;
the rules of the LORD are true,
  and righteous altogether.
More to be desired are they than gold,
  even much fine gold;
sweeter also than honey
  and drippings of the honeycomb.
Moreover, by them is your servant warned;
  in keeping them there is great reward.
Who can discern his errors?
  Declare me innocent from hidden faults.
Keep back your servant also from presumptuous sins;
  let them not have dominion over me!
Then I shall be blameless,
  and innocent of great transgression.
Let the words of my mouth and the meditation of my heart
  be acceptable in your sight,
    O LORD, my rock and my redeemer.

PRAYER OF ILLUMINATION

Strengthen me, O God, by the grace of Thy Holy Spirit. Grant me to be strengthened with might in the inner man, and to empty my heart of all useless care and anguish. O Lord, grant me heavenly wisdom, that I may learn above all things to seek and to find Thee, above all things to relish and to love Thee, and to think of all other things as being, what indeed they are, at the disposal of Thy wisdom. Amen. (Thomas A Kempis[16])

DAILY BIBLE READING

Use the Bible Reading Plan of your choice.

DAILY INTERCESSION

Pray for:

> Missions and Evangelism
> Local church members and needs
> Global, National and Local Leaders and Issues
> Personal Needs and Holiness

THE LORD'S PRAYER

Our Father in heaven, hallowed be Your name, Your kingdom come, Your will be done, on earth as in heaven. Give us today our daily bread. Forgive us our sins, as we forgive those who sin against us. Lead us not into temptation, but deliver us from evil. For the kingdom, the power, and the glory are Yours now and forever. Amen.

DOXOLOGY

Sing or say these words out loud:

> Praise God from whom all blessings flow;
> Praise Him all creatures here below;
> Praise Him above ye heavenly hosts;
> Praise Father, Son and Holy Ghost.
> Amen.

DAY 11

CALL TO WORSHIP

Malachi 1:11
For from the rising of the sun to its setting my name will be great among the nations, and in every place incense will be offered to my name, and a pure offering. For my name will be great among the nations, says the LORD of hosts.

VOTUM

Psalm 124:8
Our help is in the name of the LORD, who made heaven and earth.

CONFESSION

O God, whose nature and property is ever to have mercy and to forgive, receive our humble petitions; and though we be tied and bound with the chain of our sins, yet let the pitifulness of Thy great mercy loose us; for the honor of Jesus Christ, our Mediator, and Advocate. Amen. (Gregory The Great)

ASSURANCE OF FORGIVENESS

Romans 6:22–23
But now that you have been set free from sin and have become slaves of God, the fruit you get leads to sanctification and its end,

eternal life. For the wages of sin is death, but the free gift of God is eternal life in Christ Jesus our Lord.

PSALM OF PRAISE

Psalm 47

Clap your hands, all peoples!
　　Shout to God with loud songs of joy!
For the LORD, the Most High, is to be feared,
　　a great king over all the earth.
He subdued peoples under us,
　　and nations under our feet.
He chose our heritage for us,
　　the pride of Jacob whom he loves. *Selah*
God has gone up with a shout,
　　the LORD with the sound of a trumpet.
Sing praises to God, sing praises!
　　Sing praises to our King, sing praises!
For God is the King of all the earth;
　　sing praises with a psalm!
God reigns over the nations;
　　God sits on his holy throne.
The princes of the peoples gather
　　as the people of the God of Abraham.
For the shields of the earth belong to God;
　　he is highly exalted!

PRAYER OF ILLUMINATION

God of our Lord Jesus Christ, the Father of glory, give me the Spirit of wisdom and of revelation in the knowledge of him, having the eyes of my heart enlightened, that I may know what is the hope to which he has called me, what is the riches of his glorious inheritance in the saints, and what is his immeasurable greatness of his power toward us who believe, according to the working of his great might that he worked in Christ when he raised him from the dead and seated him in the heavenly places, far above all rule and authority and power and dominion, and above every name that is named, not only in this age but also in the one to come. (Ephesians 1:17–21)

DAILY BIBLE READING

Use the Bible Reading Plan of your choice.

DAILY INTERCESSION

Pray for:

>   Missions and Evangelism
>   Local church members and needs
>   Global, National and Local Leaders and Issues
>   Personal Needs and Holiness

THE LORD'S PRAYER

Our Father in heaven, hallowed be Your name, Your kingdom come, Your will be done, on earth as in heaven. Give us today our

daily bread. Forgive us our sins, as we forgive those who sin against us. Lead us not into temptation, but deliver us from evil. For the kingdom, the power, and the glory are Yours now and forever. Amen.

DOXOLOGY

Sing or say these words out loud:

> Praise God from whom all blessings flow;
> Praise Him all creatures here below;
> Praise Him above ye heavenly hosts;
> Praise Father, Son and Holy Ghost.
> Amen.

DAY 12

CALL TO WORSHIP

Romans 12:1
I appeal to you therefore, brothers, by the mercies of God, to present your bodies as a living sacrifice, holy and acceptable to God, which is your spiritual worship.

VOTUM

Psalm 124:8
Our help is in the name of the LORD, who made heaven and earth.

CONFESSION

O Lord, who hast mercy upon all, take away from me my sins, and mercifully kindle in me the fire of thy Holy Spirit. Take away from me the heart of stone, and give me a heart of flesh, a heart to love and adore thee, a heart to delight in thee, to follow and to enjoy thee, for Christ's sake. (Ambrose of Milan[17])

ASSURANCE OF FORGIVENESS

Isaiah 12:2
Behold, God is my salvation; I will trust, and will not be afraid; for the LORD GOD is my strength and my song, and he has become my salvation.

PSALM OF PRAISE

Psalm 138

I give you thanks, O LORD, with my whole heart;
    before the gods I sing your praise;
I bow down toward your holy temple
        and give thanks to your name for your steadfast love and
            your faithfulness,
        for you have exalted above all things
        your name and your word.
On the day I called, you answered me;
        my strength of soul you increased.
All the kings of the earth shall give you thanks, O LORD,
        for they have heard the words of your mouth,
and they shall sing of the ways of the LORD,
        for great is the glory of the LORD.
For though the LORD is high, he regards the lowly,
        but the haughty he knows from afar.
Though I walk in the midst of trouble,
        you preserve my life;
you stretch out your hand against the wrath of my enemies,
        and your right hand delivers me.
The LORD will fulfill his purpose for me;
        your steadfast love, O LORD, endures forever.
        Do not forsake the work of your hands.

PRAYER OF ILLUMINATION

Lord, teach me Your statutes. Do not hide Your commandments
from me. Make me understand the way of Your precepts. Incline

my heart to Your testimonies and not dishonest gain. Revive me according to Your lovingkindness so that I may keep the testimony Your mouth. Establish my footsteps in Your word. I have gone astray like a sheep; seek Your servant. Amen. (Psalm 119:12, 19, 27, 36, 88, 133, 176)

DAILY BIBLE READING

Use the Bible Reading Plan of your choice.

DAILY INTERCESSION

Pray for:

Missions and Evangelism
Local church members and needs
Global, National and Local Leaders and Issues
Personal Needs and Holiness

THE LORD'S PRAYER

Our Father in heaven, hallowed be Your name, Your kingdom come, Your will be done, on earth as in heaven. Give us today our daily bread. Forgive us our sins, as we forgive those who sin against us. Lead us not into temptation, but deliver us from evil. For the kingdom, the power, and the glory are Yours now and forever. Amen.

DOXOLOGY

Sing or say these words out loud:

> Praise God from whom all blessings flow;
> Praise Him all creatures here below;
> Praise Him above ye heavenly hosts;
> Praise Father, Son and Holy Ghost.
> Amen.

DAY 13

CALL TO WORSHIP

1 Chronicles 16:8-10
Oh give thanks to the LORD; call upon his name; make known his deeds among the peoples! Sing to him, sing praises to him; tell of all his wondrous works! Glory in his holy name; let the hearts of those who seek the LORD rejoice!

VOTUM

Psalm 124:8
Our help is in the name of the LORD, who made heaven and earth.

CONFESSION

I, a poor sinful man, confess before you, my Lord God and Maker, that sadly I have sinned much, with my sense, thoughts, words, and deeds, as you, eternal God, know very well. I regret them and beg your grace. Amen. (Heinrich Bullinger[18])

ASSURANCE OF FORGIVENESS

1 Peter 1:3-5
Blessed be the God and Father of our Lord Jesus Christ! According to his great mercy, he has caused us to be born again to a living hope through the resurrection of Jesus Christ from the dead, to an inheritance that is imperishable, undefiled, and unfading,

kept in heaven for you, who by God's power are being guarded through faith for a salvation ready to be revealed in the last time.

PSALM OF PRAISE

Psalm 93
The LORD reigns; he is robed in majesty;
    the LORD is robed; he has put on strength as his belt.
Yes, the world is established; it shall never be moved.
Your throne is established from of old;
    you are from everlasting.
The floods have lifted up, O LORD,
    the floods have lifted up their voice;
    the floods lift up their roaring.
Mightier than the thunders of many waters,
    mightier than the waves of the sea,
    the LORD on high is mighty!
Your decrees are very trustworthy;
    holiness befits your house,
    O LORD, forevermore.

PRAYER OF ILLUMINATION

O Highest Heavenly Father, pour into our hearts through Thy Son Jesus Christ such a light, that we may know thereby which messenger we are to obey, so that with good conscience we may lay aside the burdens of others, and may serve Thee, Eternal Heavenly Father, with free and joyful heart. Amen. (Albrecht Durer[19])

DAILY BIBLE READING

Use the Bible Reading Plan of your choice.

DAILY INTERCESSION

Pray for:

Missions and Evangelism
Local church members and needs
Global, National and Local Leaders and Issues
Personal Needs and Holiness

THE LORD'S PRAYER

Our Father in heaven, hallowed be Your name, Your kingdom come, Your will be done, on earth as in heaven. Give us today our daily bread. Forgive us our sins, as we forgive those who sin against us. Lead us not into temptation, but deliver us from evil. For the kingdom, the power, and the glory are Yours now and forever. Amen.

DOXOLOGY

Sing or say these words out loud:

Praise God from whom all blessings flow;
Praise Him all creatures here below;
Praise Him above ye heavenly hosts;
Praise Father, Son and Holy Ghost.
Amen.

DAY 14

CALL TO WORSHIP

2 Corinthians 1:3–4
Blessed be the God and Father of our Lord Jesus Christ, the Father
of mercies and God of all comfort, who comforts us in all our
affliction, so that we may be able to comfort those who are in any
affliction, with the comfort with which we ourselves are
comforted by God.

VOTUM

Psalm 124:8
Our help is in the name of the LORD, who made heaven and earth.

CONFESSION

O Lord, the great and awesome God, who keeps covenant and
steadfast love with those who love Him and keep His
commandments, we have sinned and done wrong and acted
wickedly and rebelled, turning aside from Your commandments
and rules. Amen. (Daniel 9:4–5)

ASSURANCE OF FORGIVENESS

John 6:37–39
All that the Father gives me will come to me, and whoever comes
to me I will never cast out. For I have come down from heaven,

not to do my own will but the will of him who sent me. And this is the will of him who sent me, that I should lose nothing of all that he has given me, but raise it up on the last day.

PSALM OF PRAISE

Psalm 99
The LORD reigns; let the peoples tremble!
    He sits enthroned upon the cherubim; let the earth quake!
The LORD is great in Zion;
    he is exalted over all the peoples.
Let them praise your great and awesome name!
    Holy is he!
The King in his might loves justice.
    You have established equity;
you have executed justice
    and righteousness in Jacob.
Exalt the LORD our God;
    worship at his footstool!
    Holy is he!
Moses and Aaron were among his priests,
    Samuel also was among those who called upon his name.
    They called to the LORD, and he answered them.
In the pillar of the cloud he spoke to them;
    they kept his testimonies
    and the statute that he gave them.
O LORD our God, you answered them;
    you were a forgiving God to them,
    but an avenger of their wrongdoings.

Exalt the LORD our God,
and worship at his holy mountain;
for the LORD our God is holy!

PRAYER OF ILLUMINATION

Almighty and eternal God, we pray that You would uphold us through the right knowledge of Your divine Word through Your Holy Spirit. Grant us peace and health as we do the work of our callings with Your blessing; through Your dear Son, Jesus Christ our Lord. Amen. (Martin Luther[20])

DAILY BIBLE READING

Use the Bible Reading Plan of your choice.

DAILY INTERCESSION

Pray for:

Missions and Evangelism
Local church members and needs
Global, National and Local Leaders and Issues
Personal Needs and Holiness

THE LORD'S PRAYER

Our Father in heaven, hallowed be Your name, Your kingdom come, Your will be done, on earth as in heaven. Give us today our daily bread. Forgive us our sins, as we forgive those who sin against us. Lead us not into temptation, but deliver us from evil.

For the kingdom, the power, and the glory are Yours now and forever. Amen.

DOXOLOGY

Sing or say these words out loud:

> Praise God from whom all blessings flow;
> Praise Him all creatures here below;
> Praise Him above ye heavenly hosts;
> Praise Father, Son and Holy Ghost.
> Amen.

Day 15

CALL TO WORSHIP

Psalm 18:2-3
The LORD is my rock and my fortress and my deliverer,
    my God, my rock, in whom I take refuge,
    my shield, and the horn of my salvation, my stronghold.
I call upon the LORD, who is worthy to be praised,
    and I am saved from my enemies.

VOTUM

Psalm 124:8
Our help is in the name of the LORD, who made heaven and earth.

CONFESSION

I am a poor, weak creature, and I fear I will never be able to bear testimony of the truth of Jesus Christ. But You have said, "I will give my two witnesses." I am one of Your witnesses. Now then, Lord, give power to me, for I am poor. I see the sinfulness of sin, so let me also see the graciousness of grace, and the fullness of Christ. I come to You for righteousness, because I see my sin is exceedingly sinful. O Lord, keep my soul in the ocean of Your free love. Amen. (William Bridge[21])

ASSURANCE OF FORGIVENESS

Micah 7:18–19

Who is a God like you, pardoning iniquity and passing over transgression for the remnant of his inheritance? He does not retain his anger forever, because he delights in steadfast love. He will again have compassion on us; he will tread our iniquities underfoot. You will cast all our sins into the depths of the sea.

PSALM OF PRAISE

Psalm 111

Praise the LORD!

I will give thanks to the LORD with my whole heart,
    in the company of the upright, in the congregation.
Great are the works of the LORD,
    studied by all who delight in them.
Full of splendor and majesty is his work,
    and his righteousness endures forever.
He has caused his wondrous works to be remembered;
    the LORD is gracious and merciful.
He provides food for those who fear him;
    he remembers his covenant forever.
He has shown his people the power of his works,
    in giving them the inheritance of the nations.
The works of his hands are faithful and just;
    all his precepts are trustworthy;
they are established forever and ever,
    to be performed with faithfulness and uprightness.

He sent redemption to his people;
    he has commanded his covenant forever.
    Holy and awesome is his name!
The fear of the LORD is the beginning of wisdom;
    all those who practice it have a good understanding.
    His praise endures forever!

PRAYER OF ILLUMINATION

O, make Thy Word a swift Word, passing from the ear to the heart, from the heart to lip and conversation; that, as the rain returns not empty, so neither may Thy Word, but accomplish that for which it is given. Amen. (George Herbert[22])

DAILY BIBLE READING

Use the Bible Reading Plan of your choice.

DAILY INTERCESSION

Pray for:

    Missions and Evangelism
    Local church members and needs
    Global, National and Local Leaders and Issues
    Personal Needs and Holiness

THE LORD'S PRAYER

Our Father in heaven, hallowed be Your name, Your kingdom come, Your will be done, on earth as in heaven. Give us today our

daily bread. Forgive us our sins, as we forgive those who sin against us. Lead us not into temptation, but deliver us from evil. For the kingdom, the power, and the glory are Yours now and forever. Amen.

DOXOLOGY

Sing or say these words out loud:

Praise God from whom all blessings flow;
Praise Him all creatures here below;
Praise Him above ye heavenly hosts;
Praise Father, Son and Holy Ghost.
Amen.

DAY 16

CALL TO WORSHIP

Isaiah 55:6–7
Seek the LORD while he may be found; call upon him while he is near; let the wicked forsake his way, and the unrighteous man his thoughts; let him return to the LORD, that he may have compassion on him, and to our God, for he will abundantly pardon.

VOTUM

Psalm 124:8
Our help is in the name of the LORD, who made heaven and earth.

CONFESSION

O my God, I am ashamed and blush to lift my face to you, my God, for our iniquities have risen higher than our heads, and our guilt has mounted up to the heavens. Amen. (Ezra 9:6)

ASSURANCE OF FORGIVENESS

Joel 2:13
Rend your hearts and not your garments. Return to the LORD your God, for he is gracious and merciful, slow to anger, and abounding in steadfast love; and he relents over disaster.

PSALM OF PRAISE

Psalm 98
Oh sing to the LORD a new song,
    for he has done marvelous things!
His right hand and his holy arm
    have worked salvation for him.
The LORD has made known his salvation;
    he has revealed his righteousness in the sight of the nations.
He has remembered his steadfast love and faithfulness
    to the house of Israel.
All the ends of the earth have seen
    the salvation of our God.
Make a joyful noise to the LORD, all the earth;
    break forth into joyous song and sing praises!
Sing praises to the LORD with the lyre,
    with the lyre and the sound of melody!
With trumpets and the sound of the horn
    make a joyful noise before the King, the LORD!
Let the sea roar, and all that fills it;
    the world and those who dwell in it!
Let the rivers clap their hands;
    let the hills sing for joy together
before the LORD, for he comes
    to judge the earth.
He will judge the world with righteousness,
    and the peoples with equity.

PRAYER OF ILLUMINATION

Come, Holy Spirit, with all your sweet and precious favor. Come, Lord, to convince and comfort me, to humble and direct me, to chill my affections to the world, and to warm them toward the Lord Jesus. Amen. (Robert Hawker[23])

DAILY BIBLE READING

Use the Bible Reading Plan of your choice.

DAILY INTERCESSION

Pray for:

Missions and Evangelism
Local church members and needs
Global, National and Local Leaders and Issues
Personal Needs and Holiness

THE LORD'S PRAYER

Our Father in heaven, hallowed be Your name, Your kingdom come, Your will be done, on earth as in heaven. Give us today our daily bread. Forgive us our sins, as we forgive those who sin against us. Lead us not into temptation, but deliver us from evil. For the kingdom, the power, and the glory are Yours now and forever. Amen.

DOXOLOGY

Sing or say these words out loud:

> Praise God from whom all blessings flow;
> Praise Him all creatures here below;
> Praise Him above ye heavenly hosts;
> Praise Father, Son and Holy Ghost.
> Amen.

DAY 17

CALL TO WORSHIP

Psalm 33:1-4
Shout for joy in the LORD, O you righteous!
   Praise befits the upright.
Give thanks to the LORD with the lyre;
   make melody to him with the harp of ten strings!
Sing to him a new song;
   play skillfully on the strings, with loud shouts.
For the word of the LORD is upright,
   and all his work is done in faithfulness.

VOTUM

Psalm 124:8
Our help is in the name of the LORD, who made heaven and earth.

CONFESSION

O eternal God, and most merciful Father, we confess and acknowledge before your Divine Majesty, that we are miserable sinners, conceived and born in sin and iniquity, so that there is no goodness in us. For the flesh constantly rebels against the spirit, so that we continually transgress your holy precepts and commandments, and so purchase death and damnation to ourselves through your just judgment. Nevertheless, O heavenly Father, since you have promised to offer pardon to all that repent, and seek it in the name of your beloved Son, Christ Jesus, and that by your grace we are displeased with ourselves for the sins we have committed against you, and truly repent of the same, we most humbly ask you, for Jesus Christ's sake, to show mercy to us. Amen. (Middelburg Liturgy[24])

ASSURANCE OF FORGIVENESS

Romans 5:6–8
For while we were still weak, at the right time Christ died for the ungodly. For one will scarcely die for a righteous person—though perhaps for a good person one would dare even to die—but God shows his love for us in that while we were still sinners, Christ died for us.

PSALM OF PRAISE

Psalm 104:1–12
Bless the LORD, O my soul!
    O LORD my God, you are very great!
You are clothed with splendor and majesty,
        covering yourself with light as with a garment,
        stretching out the heavens like a tent.
He lays the beams of his chambers on the waters;
he makes the clouds his chariot;
        he rides on the wings of the wind;
he makes his messengers winds,
        his ministers a flaming fire.
He set the earth on its foundations,
        so that it should never be moved.

You covered it with the deep as with a garment;
    the waters stood above the mountains.
At your rebuke they fled;
    at the sound of your thunder they took to flight.
The mountains rose, the valleys sank down
    to the place that you appointed for them.
You set a boundary that they may not pass,
    so that they might not again cover the earth.
You make springs gush forth in the valleys;
    they flow between the hills;
they give drink to every beast of the field;
    the wild donkeys quench their thirst.
Beside them the birds of the heavens dwell;
    they sing among the branches.

PRAYER OF ILLUMINATION

The Lord bless us now, and all His chosen people. Our soul crieth out for it. Break, O everlasting morning, break o'er the hills! Let our eyes behold Thee, and till the day break and the shadows flee away, abide with us, O our Beloved, abide with us now. Amen. (Charles Spurgeon[25])

DAILY BIBLE READING

Use the Bible Reading Plan of your choice.

DAILY INTERCESSION

Pray for:

Missions and Evangelism
Local church members and needs
Global, National and Local Leaders and Issues
Personal Needs and Holiness

THE LORD'S PRAYER

Our Father in heaven, hallowed be Your name, Your kingdom come, Your will be done, on earth as in heaven. Give us today our daily bread. Forgive us our sins, as we forgive those who sin against us. Lead us not into temptation, but deliver us from evil. For the kingdom, the power, and the glory are Yours now and forever. Amen.

DOXOLOGY

Sing or say these words out loud:

Praise God from whom all blessings flow;
Praise Him all creatures here below;
Praise Him above ye heavenly hosts;
Praise Father, Son and Holy Ghost.
Amen.

DAY 18

CALL TO WORSHIP

Romans 11:33–36
Oh, the depth of the riches and wisdom and knowledge of God! How unsearchable are his judgments and how inscrutable his ways! "For who has known the mind of the Lord, or who has been his counselor?" "Or who has given a gift to him that he might be repaid?" For from him and through him and to him are all things. To him be glory forever. Amen.

VOTUM

Psalm 124:8
Our help is in the name of the LORD, who made heaven and earth.

CONFESSION

O Lord, do not restrain your mercy from me; may your steadfast love and your faithfulness ever preserve me! For evils have encompassed me beyond number; my iniquities have overtaken me, and I cannot see; they are more than the hairs of my head; my heart fails me. Be pleased, O Lord, to deliver me! O Lord, make haste to help me! Amen. (Psalm 40:11–13)

ASSURANCE OF FORGIVENESS

2 Chronicles 30:9
For if you return to the LORD, your brothers and your children will find compassion with their captors and return to this land. For the LORD your God is gracious and merciful and will not turn away his face from you, if you return to him.

PSALM OF PRAISE

Psalm 104:13–23
From your lofty abode you water the mountains;
> the earth is satisfied with the fruit of your work.
You cause the grass to grow for the livestock
> and plants for man to cultivate,
that he may bring forth food from the earth
> and wine to gladden the heart of man,
oil to make his face shine
> and bread to strengthen man's heart.
The trees of the LORD are watered abundantly,
> the cedars of Lebanon that he planted.
In them the birds build their nests;
> the stork has her home in the fir trees.
The high mountains are for the wild goats;
> the rocks are a refuge for the rock badgers.
He made the moon to mark the seasons;
> the sun knows its time for setting.
You make darkness, and it is night,
> when all the beasts of the forest creep about.

The young lions roar for their prey,
    seeking their food from God.
When the sun rises, they steal away
    and lie down in their dens.
Man goes out to his work
    and to his labor until the evening.

PRAYER OF ILLUMINATION

O God in heaven, have mercy on us! Lord Jesus Christ, intercede for your people, deliver us at the opportune time, preserve in us the true genuine Christian faith, collect your scattered sheep with your voice, your divine Word as Holy Writ calls it. Help us to recognize your voice, help us not to be allured by the madness of the world, so that we may never fall away from you, O Lord Jesus Christ. Amen. (Albrecht Durer[26])

DAILY BIBLE READING

Use the Bible Reading Plan of your choice.

DAILY INTERCESSION

Pray for:

    Missions and Evangelism
    Local church members and needs
    Global, National and Local Leaders and Issues
    Personal Needs and Holiness

THE LORD'S PRAYER

Our Father in heaven, hallowed be Your name, Your kingdom come, Your will be done, on earth as in heaven. Give us today our daily bread. Forgive us our sins, as we forgive those who sin against us. Lead us not into temptation, but deliver us from evil. For the kingdom, the power, and the glory are Yours now and forever. Amen.

DOXOLOGY

Sing or say these words out loud:

> Praise God from whom all blessings flow;
> Praise Him all creatures here below;
> Praise Him above ye heavenly hosts;
> Praise Father, Son and Holy Ghost.
> Amen.

DAY 19

CALL TO WORSHIP

Revelation 15:3-4
And they sing the song of Moses, the servant of God, and the song
of the Lamb, saying, "Great and amazing are your deeds, O Lord
God the Almighty! Just and true are your ways, O King of the
nations! Who will not fear, O Lord, and glorify your name? For
you alone are holy. All nations will come and worship you, for
your righteous acts have been revealed."

VOTUM

Psalm 124:8
Our help is in the name of the LORD, who made heaven and earth.

CONFESSION

I am a poor, weak creature; unstable as water, I cannot excel.
This corruption is too hard for me, and is at the very door of
ruining my soul; and what to do I know not. My soul is become
as parched ground, and an habitation of dragons. I have made
promises and broken them; vows and engagements have been as
a thing of naught. Many persuasions have I had that I had got the
victory and should be delivered, but I am deceived; so that I
plainly see, that without some eminent succor and assistance, I
am lost, and shall be prevailed on to an utter relinquishment of
God. But yet, though this be my state and condition, let the hands

that hang down be lifted up, and the feeble knees be strengthened. Behold, the Lord Christ, that has all fullness of grace in his heart [John 1:16], all fullness of power in his hand [Matt. 28:18], he is able to slay all these his enemies. There is sufficient provision in him for my relief and assistance. He can take my drooping, dying soul and make me more than a conqueror. Amen. (John Owen[27])

ASSURANCE OF FORGIVENESS

Ephesians 1:7–8
In him we have redemption through his blood, the forgiveness of our trespasses, according to the riches of his grace, which he lavished upon us, in all wisdom and insight

PSALM OF PRAISE

Psalm 104:24–35
O LORD, how manifold are your works!
    In wisdom have you made them all;
    the earth is full of your creatures.
Here is the sea, great and wide,
    which teems with creatures innumerable,
    living things both small and great.
There go the ships,
    and Leviathan, which you formed to play in it.
These all look to you,
    to give them their food in due season.
When you give it to them, they gather it up;
    when you open your hand, they are filled with good things.

When you hide your face, they are dismayed;
when you take away their breath, they die
and return to their dust.
When you send forth your Spirit, they are created,
and you renew the face of the ground.
May the glory of the LORD endure forever;
may the LORD rejoice in his works,
who looks on the earth and it trembles,
who touches the mountains and they smoke!
I will sing to the LORD as long as I live;
I will sing praise to my God while I have being.
May my meditation be pleasing to him,
for I rejoice in the LORD.
Let sinners be consumed from the earth,
and let the wicked be no more!
Bless the LORD, O my soul!
Praise the LORD!

PRAYER OF ILLUMINATION

Dear God, let your Word shine in our hearts by your Holy Spirit. Make it so bright and warm that we always find our comfort and joy in it. Amen. (Martin Luther[28])

DAILY BIBLE READING

Use the Bible Reading Plan of your choice.

DAILY INTERCESSION

Pray for:

> Missions and Evangelism
> Local church members and needs
> Global, National and Local Leaders and Issues
> Personal Needs and Holiness

THE LORD'S PRAYER

Our Father in heaven, hallowed be Your name, Your kingdom come, Your will be done, on earth as in heaven. Give us today our daily bread. Forgive us our sins, as we forgive those who sin against us. Lead us not into temptation, but deliver us from evil. For the kingdom, the power, and the glory are Yours now and forever. Amen.

DOXOLOGY

Sing or say these words out loud:

> Praise God from whom all blessings flow;
> Praise Him all creatures here below;
> Praise Him above ye heavenly hosts;
> Praise Father, Son and Holy Ghost.
> Amen.

DAY 20

CALL TO WORSHIP

Philippians 2:9-11
Therefore God has highly exalted him and bestowed on him the name that is above every name, so that at the name of Jesus every knee should bow, in heaven and on earth and under the earth, and every tongue confess that Jesus Christ is Lord, to the glory of God the Father.

VOTUM

Psalm 124:8
Our help is in the name of the LORD, who made heaven and earth.

CONFESSION

Lord, we must sorrowfully also lament our hearts, how they wander. If Thou givest us a blessing we begin to idolize it. How often do we set our hearts upon children, upon some beloved object, or upon wealth or upon honor. Somehow or other, this spiritual adultery too often comes upon us, and the chastity of our hearts towards our God is violated. Be pleased to forgive us in this thing also. *'Take this poor heart and let it be, Forever closed to all but Thee-'* a spring shut up, a fountain sealed. Let the whole heart be Christ's alone, and never stray again. (Charles Spurgeon[29])

ASSURANCE OF FORGIVENESS

1 John 1:9
If we confess our sins, he is faithful and just to forgive us our sins
and to cleanse us from all unrighteousness.

PSALM OF PRAISE

Psalm 30
I will extol you, O LORD, for you have drawn me up
    and have not let my foes rejoice over me.
O LORD my God, I cried to you for help,
    and you have healed me.
O LORD, you have brought up my soul from Sheol;
    you restored me to life from among those who go down
        to the pit.
Sing praises to the LORD, O you his saints,
    and give thanks to his holy name.
For his anger is but for a moment,
    and his favor is for a lifetime.
Weeping may tarry for the night,
    but joy comes with the morning.
As for me, I said in my prosperity,
    "I shall never be moved."
By your favor, O LORD,
    you made my mountain stand strong;
you hid your face;
    I was dismayed.
To you, O LORD, I cry,
    and to the Lord I plead for mercy:

"What profit is there in my death,
    if I go down to the pit?
Will the dust praise you?
    Will it tell of your faithfulness?
Hear, O LORD, and be merciful to me!
    O LORD, be my helper!"
You have turned for me my mourning into dancing;
    you have loosed my sackcloth
    and clothed me with gladness,
that my glory may sing your praise and not be silent.
    O LORD my God, I will give thanks to you forever!

PRAYER OF ILLUMINATION

Be all I need, dearest Lord. Let me hear your voice and see your countenance. Because both in life and in death, in time and to all eternity, the voice of my Lord Jesus will be my everlasting comfort. No one speaks like you! Amen. (Robert Hawker[30])

DAILY BIBLE READING

Use the Bible Reading Plan of your choice.

DAILY INTERCESSION

Pray for:

Missions and Evangelism
Local church members and needs

Global, National and Local Leaders and Issues
Personal Needs and Holiness

THE LORD'S PRAYER

Our Father in heaven, hallowed be Your name, Your kingdom come, Your will be done, on earth as in heaven. Give us today our daily bread. Forgive us our sins, as we forgive those who sin against us. Lead us not into temptation, but deliver us from evil. For the kingdom, the power, and the glory are Yours now and forever. Amen.

DOXOLOGY

Sing or say these words out loud:
Praise God from whom all blessings flow;
Praise Him all creatures here below;
Praise Him above ye heavenly hosts;
Praise Father, Son and Holy Ghost.
Amen.

DAY 21

CALL TO WORSHIP

Colossians 1:15–17
He is the image of the invisible God, the firstborn of all creation. For by him all things were created, in heaven and on earth, visible and invisible, whether thrones or dominions or rulers or authorities—all things were created through him and for him. And he is before all things, and in him all things hold together.

VOTUM

Psalm 124:8
Our help is in the name of the LORD, who made heaven and earth.

CONFESSION

To us, O LORD, belongs open shame, to our kings, to our princes, and to our fathers, because we have sinned against You. To You, the Lord our God, belong mercy and forgiveness. We have rebelled against You and have not obeyed the voice of the LORD our God by walking in Your laws, which You set before us by Your servants the prophets. All of Your people have transgressed Your law and turned aside, refusing to obey Your voice. And the curse and oath that are written in the Law of Moses the servant of God have been poured out upon us, because we have sinned against You. Amen. (Daniel 9:8–11)

ASSURANCE OF FORGIVENESS

Colossians 1:21–22
And you, who once were alienated and hostile in mind, doing evil deeds, he has now reconciled in his body of flesh by his death, in order to present you holy and blameless and above reproach before him.

PSALM OF PRAISE

Psalm 33:1–11
Shout for joy in the LORD, O you righteous!
    Praise befits the upright.
Give thanks to the LORD with the lyre;
    make melody to him with the harp of ten strings!
Sing to him a new song;
    play skillfully on the strings, with loud shouts.
For the word of the LORD is upright,
    and all his work is done in faithfulness.
He loves righteousness and justice;
    the earth is full of the steadfast love of the LORD.
By the word of the LORD the heavens were made,
    and by the breath of his mouth all their host.
He gathers the waters of the sea as a heap;
    he puts the deeps in storehouses.
Let all the earth fear the LORD;
    let all the inhabitants of the world stand in awe of him!
For he spoke, and it came to be;
    he commanded, and it stood firm.

The LORD brings the counsel of the nations to nothing;
    he frustrates the plans of the peoples.
The counsel of the LORD stands forever,
    the plans of his heart to all generations.

PRAYER OF ILLUMINATION

Almighty God, unto whom all hearts are open, all desires known, and from whom no secrets are hid; Cleanse the thoughts of our hearts by the inspiration of thy Holy Spirit, that we may perfectly love thee, and worthily magnify thy holy Name; through Christ our Lord. Amen. (*The Book of Common Prayer*, 1789)

DAILY BIBLE READING

Use the Bible Reading Plan of your choice.

DAILY INTERCESSION

Pray for:

    Missions and Evangelism
    Local church members and needs
    Global, National and Local Leaders and Issues
    Personal Needs and Holiness

THE LORD'S PRAYER

Our Father in heaven, hallowed be Your name, Your kingdom come, Your will be done, on earth as in heaven. Give us today our

daily bread. Forgive us our sins, as we forgive those who sin against us. Lead us not into temptation, but deliver us from evil. For the kingdom, the power, and the glory are Yours now and forever. Amen.

DOXOLOGY

Sing or say these words out loud:

> Praise God from whom all blessings flow;
> Praise Him all creatures here below;
> Praise Him above ye heavenly hosts;
> Praise Father, Son and Holy Ghost. Amen.

DAY 22

CALL TO WORSHIP

Revelation 4:11
Worthy are you, our Lord and God, to receive glory and honor and power, for you created all things, and by your will they existed and were created.

VOTUM

Psalm 124:8
Our help is in the name of the LORD, who made heaven and earth.

CONFESSION

Father, by the disobedience of Adam ,original sin has been spread through the whole human race. It is a corruption of the whole human nature— an inherited depravity which even infects small infants in their mother's womb, and the root which produces in humanity every sort of sin. It is so vile and enormous in God's sight that it is enough to condemn the human race, and it is not abolished or wholly uprooted even by baptism, seeing that sin constantly boils forth as though from a contaminated spring. Nevertheless, I ask You not to let sin be imputed to me for my condemnation, but instead forgiven by Christ's grace and mercy. Amen. (Adapted from *The Belgic Confession*, 1561[31])

ASSURANCE OF FORGIVENESS

1 John 2:2
He is the propitiation for our sins, and not for ours only but also
for the sins of the whole world.

PSALM OF PRAISE

Psalm 33:12–22
Blessed is the nation whose God is the LORD,
     the people whom he has chosen as his heritage!
The LORD looks down from heaven;
     he sees all the children of man;
from where he sits enthroned he looks out
     on all the inhabitants of the earth,
he who fashions the hearts of them all
     and observes all their deeds.
The king is not saved by his great army;
     a warrior is not delivered by his great strength.
The war horse is a false hope for salvation,
     and by its great might it cannot rescue.
Behold, the eye of the LORD is on those who fear him,
     on those who hope in his steadfast love,
that he may deliver their soul from death
     and keep them alive in famine.
Our soul waits for the LORD;
     he is our help and our shield.
For our heart is glad in him,
     because we trust in his holy name.

Let your steadfast love, O LORD, be upon us,
> even as we hope in you.

PRAYER OF ILLUMINATION

Dearest Lord God, give me your grace so that I rightly understand
your Word, and more than that, that I also do what it says. O
dearest Lord Jesus Christ, if my study is not to your glory alone,
then do not let me understand even the smallest letter. Give me
only as much understanding as a poor sinner needs for your
glory. Amen. (Martin Luther[32])

DAILY BIBLE READING

Use the Bible Reading Plan of your choice.

DAILY INTERCESSION

Pray for:

> Missions and Evangelism
> Local church members and needs
> Global, National and Local Leaders and Issues
> Personal Needs and Holiness

THE LORD'S PRAYER

Our Father in heaven, hallowed be Your name, Your kingdom
come, Your will be done, on earth as in heaven. Give us today our
daily bread. Forgive us our sins, as we forgive those who sin
against us. Lead us not into temptation, but deliver us from evil.

For the kingdom, the power, and the glory are Yours now and forever. Amen.

DOXOLOGY

Sing or say these words out loud:

> Praise God from whom all blessings flow;
> Praise Him all creatures here below;
> Praise Him above ye heavenly hosts;
> Praise Father, Son and Holy Ghost.
> Amen.

DAY 23

CALL TO WORSHIP

2 Corinthians 1:3–4
Blessed be the God and Father of our Lord Jesus Christ, the Father of mercies and God of all comfort, who comforts us in all our affliction, so that we may be able to comfort those who are in any affliction, with the comfort with which we ourselves are comforted by God.

VOTUM

Psalm 124:8
Our help is in the name of the LORD, who made heaven and earth.

CONFESSION

What! Lord! after all that I have done, after my base returns, my repeated wanderings, my aggravated transgressions, my complicated iniquity, my sins against conviction, light, and love do You still stretch out your hand to me, a poor wretched wanderer as I am? Do You go forth to meet, to welcome, to pardon me? Do You watch the first kindling of penitence, the first tear of contrition, the first word of confession, 'Father, I have sinned!' Lord, I fall at Your feet, the greatest of sinners. Your power has drawn me, Your love has subdued me, Your grace has conquered me! Amen. (Octavius Winslow[33])

ASSURANCE OF FORGIVENESS

Jeremiah 31:31–34

Behold, the days are coming, declares the LORD, when I will make a new covenant with the house of Israel and the house of Judah, not like the covenant that I made with their fathers on the day when I took them by the hand to bring them out of the land of Egypt, my covenant that they broke, though I was their husband, declares the LORD. For this is the covenant that I will make with the house of Israel after those days, declares the LORD: I will put my law within them, and I will write it on their hearts. And I will be their God, and they shall be my people. And no longer shall each one teach his neighbor and each his brother, saying, 'Know the LORD,' for they shall all know me, from the least of them to the greatest, declares the LORD. For I will forgive their iniquity, and I will remember their sin no more.

PSALM OF PRAISE

Psalm 119:7, 62, 108, 164, 171, 175
I will praise you with an upright heart,
    when I learn your righteous rules. ...
At midnight I rise to praise you,
    because of your righteous rules. ...
Accept my freewill offerings of praise, O LORD,
    and teach me your rules. ...
Seven times a day I praise you
    for your righteous rules. ...
My lips will pour forth praise,
    for you teach me your statutes. ...

Let my soul live and praise you,
and let your rules help me.

PRAYER OF ILLUMINATION

May that good Spirit of Jesus Christ open the eyes of our minds, that we may see and approve things that are excellent. May he persuade our hearts to receive the truth in the love of it, and direct our steps to walk in the paths of mercy and truth, that we may be saved. Amen. (William Ames[34])

DAILY BIBLE READING

Use the Bible Reading Plan of your choice.

DAILY INTERCESSION

Pray for:

> Missions and Evangelism
> Local church members and needs
> Global, National and Local Leaders and Issues
> Personal Needs and Holiness

THE LORD'S PRAYER

Our Father in heaven, hallowed be Your name, Your kingdom come, Your will be done, on earth as in heaven. Give us today our daily bread. Forgive us our sins, as we forgive those who sin against us. Lead us not into temptation, but deliver us from evil.

For the kingdom, the power, and the glory are Yours now and forever. Amen.

DOXOLOGY

Sing or say these words out loud:

> Praise God from whom all blessings flow;
> Praise Him all creatures here below;
> Praise Him above ye heavenly hosts;
> Praise Father, Son and Holy Ghost.
> Amen.

DAY 24

CALL TO WORSHIP

Isaiah 6:1–3

In the year that King Uzziah died I saw the Lord sitting upon a throne, high and lifted up; and the train of his robe filled the temple. Above him stood the seraphim. Each had six wings: with two he covered his face, and with two he covered his feet, and with two he flew. And one called to another and said: "Holy, holy, holy is the LORD of hosts; the whole earth is full of his glory!"

VOTUM

Psalm 124:8

Our help is in the name of the LORD, who made heaven and earth.

CONFESSION

Injured King and Almighty Judge, what can I say to the charges against me? Should I pretend to be offended, and defend myself? I do not dare. You know my foolishness. None of my sins is hidden from You. I am more guilty than I can say. What has my life been but rebellion against You? It is not this or that particular sin alone. From start to finish, nothing has been right. My whole soul has been disordered. But if there is yet any way of deliverance, any hope for so guilty a creature, may it be opened to me by your Gospel and grace. Amen. (Phillip Doddridge[35])

ASSURANCE OF FORGIVENESS

Titus 3:4–7
But when the goodness and loving kindness of God our Savior appeared, he saved us, not because of works done by us in righteousness, but according to his own mercy, by the washing of regeneration and renewal of the Holy Spirit, whom he poured out on us richly through Jesus Christ our Savior, so that being justified by his grace we might become heirs according to the hope of eternal life.

PSALM OF PRAISE

Psalm 117
Praise the LORD, all nations!
    Extol him, all peoples!
For great is his steadfast love toward us,
    and the faithfulness of the LORD endures forever.
Praise the LORD!

PRAYER OF ILLUMINATION

Behold, Lord, my heart lies exposed before You. Open the ears of that heart and say unto my soul, "I am your salvation." After You have spoken, allow me to quickly grasp you. Hide not Your face from me. (Augustine[36])

DAILY BIBLE READING

Use the Bible Reading Plan of your choice.

DAILY INTERCESSION

Pray for:

Missions and Evangelism
Local church members and needs
Global, National and Local Leaders and Issues
Personal Needs and Holiness

THE LORD'S PRAYER

Our Father in heaven, hallowed be Your name, Your kingdom come, Your will be done, on earth as in heaven. Give us today our daily bread. Forgive us our sins, as we forgive those who sin against us. Lead us not into temptation, but deliver us from evil. For the kingdom, the power, and the glory are Yours now and forever. Amen.

DOXOLOGY

Sing or say these words out loud:

Praise God from whom all blessings flow;
Praise Him all creatures here below;
Praise Him above ye heavenly hosts;
Praise Father, Son and Holy Ghost.
Amen.

DAY 25

CALL TO WORSHIP

Matthew 11:28-29
Come to me, all who labor and are heavy laden, and I will give
you rest. Take my yoke upon you, and learn from me, for I am
gentle and lowly in heart, and you will find rest for your souls.

VOTUM

Psalm 124:8
Our help is in the name of the LORD, who made heaven and earth.

CONFESSION

We cry to You, God, for renewing grace. We lie at Your footstool
and cry, "Help, Lord, or I will perish!" Create in me a new heart,
a renew a right spirit within me. Renew me in the spirit of my
mind, and renew me in my inner soul. Take away this old mind
that is so blind, so vain, so carnal. Take away this old will that is
so obstinate, so perverse, so rebellious. Take away this old
conscience that is so partial, so seared, so senseless. Take away
this old heart that will never delight in, comply with, or submit
to You. Let old things pass away, let all things become new.
Amen. (David Clarkson[37])

ASSURANCE OF FORGIVENESS

Hebrews 9:11–14
But when Christ appeared as a high priest of the good things that
have come, then through the greater and more perfect tent (not
made with hands, that is, not of this creation) he entered once for
all into the holy places, not by means of the blood of goats and
calves but by means of his own blood, thus securing an eternal
redemption. For if the blood of goats and bulls, and the
sprinkling of defiled persons with the ashes of a heifer, sanctify
for the purification of the flesh, how much more will the blood of
Christ, who through the eternal Spirit offered himself without
blemish to God, purify our conscience from dead works to serve
the living God.

PSALM OF PRAISE

Psalm 123
To you I lift up my eyes,
    O you who are enthroned in the heavens!
Behold, as the eyes of servants
    look to the hand of their master,
as the eyes of a maidservant
    to the hand of her mistress,
so our eyes look to the LORD our God,
    till he has mercy upon us. ...
Our soul has had more than enough
    of the scorn of those who are at ease,
    of the contempt of the proud.

PRAYER OF ILLUMINATION

Lord, open my ear to discipline. Silence my objections. Suppress the risings of the carnal mind against the Word. Make me consent to the law that is good and to esteem all the precepts concerning all things to be right even when they go against my flesh and blood. (Adapted from Matthew Henry[38])

DAILY BIBLE READING

Use the Bible Reading Plan of your choice.

DAILY INTERCESSION

Pray for:

Missions and Evangelism
Local church members and needs
Global, National and Local Leaders and Issues
Personal Needs and Holiness

THE LORD'S PRAYER

Our Father in heaven, hallowed be Your name, Your kingdom come, Your will be done, on earth as in heaven. Give us today our daily bread. Forgive us our sins, as we forgive those who sin against us. Lead us not into temptation, but deliver us from evil. For the kingdom, the power, and the glory are Yours now and forever. Amen.

DOXOLOGY

Sing or say these words out loud:

> Praise God from whom all blessings flow;
> Praise Him all creatures here below;
> Praise Him above ye heavenly hosts;
> Praise Father, Son and Holy Ghost.
> Amen.

Day 26

CALL TO WORSHIP

Micah 6:6–8

With what shall I come before the LORD, and bow myself before God on high? Shall I come before him with burnt offerings, with calves a year old? Will the LORD be pleased with thousands of rams, with ten thousands of rivers of oil? Shall I give my firstborn for my transgression, the fruit of my body for the sin of my soul?" He has told you, O man, what is good; and what does the LORD require of you but to do justice, and to love kindness, and to walk humbly with your God?

VOTUM

Psalm 124:8

Our help is in the name of the LORD, who made heaven and earth.

CONFESSION

O Lord Jesus Christ, you are the sun of the world, evermore arising, and never going down, which by your most welcome appearing and sight, brings forth, preserves, nourishes, and refreshes all things, as well that are in heaven as also that are on earth; We beg you mercifully and faithfully to shine in our hearts, so that the night and darkness of sins, and the mist of errors on every side may be driven away; with you brightly shining in our hearts we may all our life go without stumbling or

111

offense, and may decently and seemly walk as in the day time, being pure and clean from the works of darkness, and abounding in all good works which God has prepared us to walk in; you who with the Father and with the Holy Ghost live and reign for ever and ever. Amen. (Thomas Cranmer[39])

ASSURANCE OF FORGIVENESS

Matthew 1:19–21
And her husband Joseph, being a just man and unwilling to put her to shame, resolved to divorce her quietly. But as he considered these things, behold, an angel of the Lord appeared to him in a dream, saying, "Joseph, son of David, do not fear to take Mary as your wife, for that which is conceived in her is from the Holy Spirit. She will bear a son, and you shall call his name Jesus, for he will save his people from their sins."

PSALM OF PRAISE

Psalm 139:1–7
O LORD, you have searched me and known me!
You know when I sit down and when I rise up;
    you discern my thoughts from afar.
You search out my path and my lying down
    and are acquainted with all my ways.
Even before a word is on my tongue,
    behold, O LORD, you know it altogether.
You hem me in, behind and before,
    and lay your hand upon me.

Such knowledge is too wonderful for me;
it is high; I cannot attain it.
Where shall I go from your Spirit?
Or where shall I flee from your presence?

PRAYER OF ILLUMINATION

Lord God, heavenly Father, we thank you that through your Son Jesus Christ you have sown your holy Word among us. Prepare our hearts by your Holy Spirit that we may diligently and reverently hear your Word, keep it in good hearts and bring forth fruit with patience. Do not let our hearts incline to sin, but subdue them by your power and in all persecutions comfort us with your grace and continual help; through your beloved Son, Jesus Christ, our Lord, who lives and reigns with you and the Holy Spirit, ever one God, now and forever. Amen.[40]

DAILY BIBLE READING

Use the Bible Reading Plan of your choice.

DAILY INTERCESSION

Pray for:

Missions and Evangelism
Local church members and needs
Global, National and Local Leaders and Issues
Personal Needs and Holiness

THE LORD'S PRAYER

Our Father in heaven, hallowed be Your name, Your kingdom come, Your will be done, on earth as in heaven. Give us today our daily bread. Forgive us our sins, as we forgive those who sin against us. Lead us not into temptation, but deliver us from evil. For the kingdom, the power, and the glory are Yours now and forever. Amen.

DOXOLOGY

Sing or say these words out loud:

> Praise God from whom all blessings flow;
> Praise Him all creatures here below;
> Praise Him above ye heavenly hosts;
> Praise Father, Son and Holy Ghost.
> Amen.

DAY 27

CALL TO WORSHIP

Psalm 92:1–3
It is good to give thanks to the LORD,
    to sing praises to your name, O Most High;
to declare your steadfast love in the morning,
    and your faithfulness by night,
to the music of the lute and the harp,
    to the melody of the lyre.

VOTUM

Psalm 124:8
Our help is in the name of the LORD, who made heaven and earth.

CONFESSION

Lord Jesus, thou hast promised not to quench the smoking flax, nor to break the bruised reed. Cherish thy grace in me; leave me not to myself; the glory shall be thine. Let us not allow Satan to transform Christ to us, to make him other than he is to those that are his. Amen. (Richard Sibbes[41])

ASSURANCE OF FORGIVENESS

Proverbs 28:13
Whoever conceals his transgressions will not prosper,
    but he who confesses and forsakes them will obtain mercy.

PSALM OF PRAISE

Psalm 139:8–16
If I ascend to heaven, you are there!
    If I make my bed in Sheol, you are there!
If I take the wings of the morning
    and dwell in the uttermost parts of the sea,
even there your hand shall lead me,
    and your right hand shall hold me.
If I say, "Surely the darkness shall cover me,
    and the light about me be night,"
even the darkness is not dark to you;
    the night is bright as the day,
    for darkness is as light with you.
For you formed my inward parts;
    you knitted me together in my mother's womb.
I praise you, for I am fearfully and wonderfully made.
Wonderful are your works;
    my soul knows it very well.
My frame was not hidden from you,
when I was being made in secret,
    intricately woven in the depths of the earth.
Your eyes saw my unformed substance;
in your book were written, every one of them,
    the days that were formed for me,
    when as yet there was none of them.

PRAYER OF ILLUMINATION

Father, may I never be satisfied with my present spiritual progress, but to faith add virtue, knowledge, temperance, godliness, brotherly kindness, charity. May I never neglect what is necessary to constitute Christian character, and needful to complete it. May I cultivate the expedient, develop the lovely, adorn the gospel, recommend the religion of Jesus, accommodate myself to thy providence. Keep me from sinking or sinning in the evil day; Help me to carry into ordinary life portions of divine truth and use them on suitable occasions, so its doctrines may inform, its warnings caution, its rules guide, its promises comfort me. Amen. (*The Valley of Vision*[42])

DAILY BIBLE READING

Use the Bible Reading Plan of your choice.

DAILY INTERCESSION

Pray for:

> Missions and Evangelism
> Local church members and needs
> Global, National and Local Leaders and Issues
> Personal Needs and Holiness

THE LORD'S PRAYER

Our Father in heaven, hallowed be Your name, Your kingdom come, Your will be done, on earth as in heaven. Give us today our

daily bread. Forgive us our sins, as we forgive those who sin against us. Lead us not into temptation, but deliver us from evil. For the kingdom, the power, and the glory are Yours now and forever. Amen.

DOXOLOGY

Sing or say these words out loud:

> Praise God from whom all blessings flow;
> Praise Him all creatures here below;
> Praise Him above ye heavenly hosts;
> Praise Father, Son and Holy Ghost.
> Amen.

Day 28

Exodus 34:6-7
The LORD passed before him and proclaimed, "The LORD, the LORD, a God merciful and gracious, slow to anger, and abounding in steadfast love and faithfulness, keeping steadfast love for thousands, forgiving iniquity and transgression and sin, but who will by no means clear the guilty, visiting the iniquity of the fathers on the children and the children's children, to the third and the fourth generation."

VOTUM

Psalm 124:8
Our help is in the name of the LORD, who made heaven and earth.

CONFESSION

I confess, Lord, that daily tears and signs are not unsuitable to the eyes and voice of so great a sinner, now under the correcting rod. But "he that offereth praise glorifies thee," and is not this the "spiritual sacrifice, acceptable through Christ," for which we are made priests to God? I refuse not, Lord, to lie in tears and groans when thou requirest it, nor do thou reject those tears and groans; but O give me better, that I may have better of thine own to offer thee, and so prepare me for the far better which I shall find with Christ! (Richard Baxter[43])

ASSURANCE OF FORGIVENESS

Isaiah 1:18

Come now, let us reason together, says the LORD: though your sins are like scarlet, they shall be as white as snow; though they are red like crimson, they shall become like wool.

PSALM OF PRAISE

Psalm 139:17–24

How precious to me are your thoughts, O God!
    How vast is the sum of them!
If I would count them, they are more than the sand.
    I awake, and I am still with you.
Oh that you would slay the wicked, O God!
    O men of blood, depart from me!
They speak against you with malicious intent;
    your enemies take your name in vain.
Do I not hate those who hate you, O LORD?
    And do I not loathe those who rise up against you?
I hate them with complete hatred;
    I count them my enemies.
Search me, O God, and know my heart!
    Try me and know my thoughts!
And see if there be any grievous way in me,
    and lead me in the way everlasting!

PRAYER OF ILLUMINATION

O God, Father of all poor, miserable souls! Give us all your grace and enlighten us with your truth. To you be praise, glory and thanks forever. Amen. Lord Jesus, our King, you are Peace, Light and Life. Enlighten, awaken and strengthen our hearts by the power of your holy Word for eternal life. To you be praise, glory and thanks forever. Amen. (Martin Luther[44])

DAILY BIBLE READING

Use the Bible Reading Plan of your choice.

DAILY INTERCESSION

Pray for:

> Missions and Evangelism
> Local church members and needs
> Global, National and Local Leaders and Issues
> Personal Needs and Holiness

THE LORD'S PRAYER

Our Father in heaven, hallowed be Your name, Your kingdom come, Your will be done, on earth as in heaven. Give us today our daily bread. Forgive us our sins, as we forgive those who sin against us. Lead us not into temptation, but deliver us from evil. For the kingdom, the power, and the glory are Yours now and forever. Amen.

DOXOLOGY

Sing or say these words out loud:

> Praise God from whom all blessings flow;
> Praise Him all creatures here below;
> Praise Him above ye heavenly hosts;
> Praise Father, Son and Holy Ghost.
> Amen.

DAY 29

CALL TO WORSHIP

Ephesians 1:3-6
Blessed be the God and Father of our Lord Jesus Christ, who has blessed us in Christ with every spiritual blessing in the heavenly places, even as he chose us in him before the foundation of the world, that we should be holy and blameless before him. In love he predestined us for adoption to himself as sons through Jesus Christ, according to the purpose of his will, to the praise of his glorious grace, with which he has blessed us in the Beloved.

VOTUM

Psalm 124:8
Our help is in the name of the LORD, who made heaven and earth.

CONFESSION

Lord, confession of sin endears Christ to the soul. If I say I am a sinner, how precious will Christ's blood be to me! If a debtor confessed a judgment but the creditor will not exact the debt, instead appointing his own son to pay for it, will not the debtor be very thankful? So when we confess the debt, and that even though we should forever lie in hell we cannot pay it, but that God should appoint his own Son to lay down his blood for the payment of our debt, how free is grace magnified and Jesus Christ eternally loved and admired! (Thomas Watson[45])

ASSURANCE OF FORGIVENESS

Romans 4:5–8

And to the one who does not work but believes in him who justifies the ungodly, his faith is counted as righteousness, just as David also speaks of the blessing of the one to whom God counts righteousness apart from works: "Blessed are those whose lawless deeds are forgiven, and whose sins are covered; blessed is the man against whom the Lord will not count his sin.

PSALM OF PRAISE

Psalm 16

Preserve me, O God, for in you I take refuge.
I say to the LORD, "You are my Lord;
    I have no good apart from you."
As for the saints in the land, they are the excellent ones,
    in whom is all my delight.
The sorrows of those who run after another god shall multiply;
    their drink offerings of blood I will not pour out
    or take their names on my lips.
The LORD is my chosen portion and my cup;
    you hold my lot.
The lines have fallen for me in pleasant places;
    indeed, I have a beautiful inheritance.
I bless the LORD who gives me counsel;
    in the night also my heart instructs me.
I have set the LORD always before me;
    because he is at my right hand, I shall not be shaken.

Therefore my heart is glad, and my whole being rejoices;
    my flesh also dwells secure.
For you will not abandon my soul to Sheol,
    or let your holy one see corruption.
You make known to me the path of life;
    in your presence there is fullness of joy;
    at your right hand are pleasures forevermore.

PRAYER OF ILLUMINATION

Father, Your thoughts are not my thoughts, neither are Your ways my ways. You have declared this. For as the heavens are higher than the earth, so are Your ways higher than my ways and Your thoughts than my thoughts. For as the rain and the snow come down from heaven and do not return there but water the earth, making it bring forth and sprout, giving seed to the sower and bread to the eater, so shall Your word be that goes out from Your mouth; it shall not return to You empty, but it shall accomplish that which You purpose, and shall succeed in the thing for which You sent it. Amen. (Isaiah 55:8–10)

DAILY BIBLE READING

Use the Bible Reading Plan of your choice.

DAILY INTERCESSION

Pray for:

Missions and Evangelism
Local church members and needs
Global, National and Local Leaders and Issues
Personal Needs and Holiness

THE LORD'S PRAYER

Our Father in heaven, hallowed be Your name, Your kingdom come, Your will be done, on earth as in heaven. Give us today our daily bread. Forgive us our sins, as we forgive those who sin against us. Lead us not into temptation, but deliver us from evil. For the kingdom, the power, and the glory are Yours now and forever. Amen.

DOXOLOGY

Sing or say these words out loud:

Praise God from whom all blessings flow;
Praise Him all creatures here below;
Praise Him above ye heavenly hosts;
Praise Father, Son and Holy Ghost.
Amen.

Day 30

CALL TO WORSHIP

Psalm 34:3
Oh, magnify the Lord with me,
    and let us exalt his name together!

VOTUM

Psalm 124:8
Our help is in the name of the Lord, who made heaven and earth.

CONFESSION

Lord, I have not done my duty in my own family, among Christians, in the churches of Christ. I have not done what I promised. I have not served my generation or helped to build the building of Zion. And now, Lord, what can I say? Is my name written on the heart of Christ? If I had the whole world's glory, if I had ten thousand worlds, and ten thousand lives, I would lay them all down, to have my poor trembling soul assured of this. Amen. (Isaac Ambrose[46])

ASSURANCE OF FORGIVENESS

Psalm 32:5
I acknowledged my sin to you,
    and I did not cover my iniquity;

I said, "I will confess my transgressions to the LORD,"
    and you forgave the iniquity of my sin.

PSALM OF PRAISE

Psalm 146
Praise the LORD!
Praise the LORD, O my soul!
I will praise the LORD as long as I live;
    I will sing praises to my God while I have my being.
Put not your trust in princes,
    in a son of man, in whom there is no salvation.
When his breath departs, he returns to the earth;
    on that very day his plans perish.
Blessed is he whose help is the God of Jacob,
    whose hope is in the LORD his God,
who made heaven and earth,
    the sea, and all that is in them,
who keeps faith forever;
    who executes justice for the oppressed,
    who gives food to the hungry.
The LORD sets the prisoners free;
    the LORD opens the eyes of the blind.
The LORD lifts up those who are bowed down;
    the LORD loves the righteous.
The LORD watches over the sojourners;
    he upholds the widow and the fatherless,
    but the way of the wicked he brings to ruin.

The LORD will reign forever,
    your God, O Zion, to all generations.
Praise the LORD!

PRAYER OF ILLUMINATION

Have pity, O Lord, upon our weakness, and give us a better mind to understand the true sense of your word. Give us a simplicity of the heart to receive it, the integrity to declare it, and a zeal to teach and defend it. Amen. (Phillip Doddridge[47])

DAILY BIBLE READING

Use the Bible Reading Plan of your choice.

DAILY INTERCESSION

Pray for:

    Missions and Evangelism
    Local church members and needs
    Global, National and Local Leaders and Issues
    Personal Needs and Holiness

THE LORD'S PRAYER

Our Father in heaven, hallowed be Your name, Your kingdom come, Your will be done, on earth as in heaven. Give us today our daily bread. Forgive us our sins, as we forgive those who sin against us. Lead us not into temptation, but deliver us from evil.

For the kingdom, the power, and the glory are Yours now and forever. Amen.

DOXOLOGY

Sing or say these words out loud:

> Praise God from whom all blessings flow;
> Praise Him all creatures here below;
> Praise Him above ye heavenly hosts;
> Praise Father, Son and Holy Ghost.
> Amen.

DAY 31

CALL TO WORSHIP

Zephaniah 3:14-15
Sing aloud, O daughter of Zion;
   shout, O Israel!
Rejoice and exult with all your heart,
   O daughter of Jerusalem!
The LORD has taken away the judgments against you;
   he has cleared away your enemies.
The King of Israel, the LORD, is in your midst;
   you shall never again fear evil.

VOTUM

Psalm 124:8
Our help is in the name of the LORD, who made heaven and earth.

CONFESSION

Omnipotent and everlasting God, Father of our Lord Jesus Christ, who by thy eternal providence disposes kingdoms, as seemeth best to thy wisdom: we acknowledge and confess thy judgments to be righteous, in that thou hast taken from us, for our ingratitude, and for abusing of thy most holy word, our native king and earthly comforter. But, O Lord, behold thy own mercy and goodness, that thou may purge and remove the most filthy burden of our most horrible offenses. Let thy love overcome the

131

severity of thy judgments, even as it did in giving to the world thy only Son, Jesus, when all mankind was lost, and no obedience was left in Adam nor in his seed. Regenerate our hearts, O Lord, by the strength of thy Holy Ghost. Convert thou us, and we shall be converted. Work thou in us unfeigned repentance, and move thou our hearts to obey thy holy laws. (John Knox[48])

ASSURANCE OF FORGIVENESS

Acts 3:19–21
Repent therefore, and turn back, that your sins may be blotted out, that times of refreshing may come from the presence of the Lord, and that he may send the Christ appointed for you, Jesus, whom heaven must receive until the time for restoring all the things about which God spoke by the mouth of his holy prophets long ago.

PSALM OF PRAISE

Psalm 23
The LORD is my shepherd; I shall not want.
　　He makes me lie down in green pastures.
He leads me beside still waters.
　　He restores my soul.
He leads me in paths of righteousness
　　for his name's sake.
Even though I walk through the valley of the shadow of death,
　　I will fear no evil,
for you are with me;
　　your rod and your staff, they comfort me.

You prepare a table before me
    in the presence of my enemies;
you anoint my head with oil;
    my cup overflows.
Surely goodness and mercy shall follow me
    all the days of my life,
and I shall dwell in the house of the LORD forever.

PRAYER OF ILLUMINATION

Lord, I am now entering into your presence, to hear you speak from heaven to me, to receive your rain and spiritual dew, which never return in vain, but ripen a harvest either of corn or weeds, of grace or judgment. My heart is prepared, O Lord, my heart is prepared to learn and to love any of your words. Your law is my counselor; I will be ruled by it. It is my physician; I will be a patient under it. It is my schoolmaster; I will be obedient to it. Be therefore please to reveal your own Spirit to me, and to work in me that which your require. (Edward Reynolds[49])

DAILY BIBLE READING

Use the Bible Reading Plan of your choice.

DAILY INTERCESSION

Pray for:

    Missions and Evangelism
    Local church members and needs

Global, National and Local Leaders and Issues
Personal Needs and Holiness

THE LORD'S PRAYER

Our Father in heaven, hallowed be Your name, Your kingdom come, Your will be done, on earth as in heaven. Give us today our daily bread. Forgive us our sins, as we forgive those who sin against us. Lead us not into temptation, but deliver us from evil. For the kingdom, the power, and the glory are Yours now and forever. Amen.

DOXOLOGY

Sing or say these words out loud:

Praise God from whom all blessings flow;
Praise Him all creatures here below;
Praise Him above ye heavenly hosts;
Praise Father, Son and Holy Ghost.
Amen.

APPENDIX

In this appendix, you will find multiple alternate liturgies to be used at the beginning of special seasons and on special days. There are liturgies for the following occasions:

- Beginning of Advent: The season of spiritual preparation that leads to Christmas. It begins on the fourth Sunday before Christmas day.
- Christmas: The celebration of the birth of Christ.
- Epiphany: The celebration of Christ being revealed to Gentiles. It is observed on January 6th—twelve days after Christmas day.
- Lent: The season of spiritual preparation that leads to Good Friday and Easter. It begins on Ash Wednesday and lasts until sundown on the Thursday before Easter.
- Good Friday: The day that we remember the sacrifice of Christ on the Cross.
- Easter: The celebration of the resurrection of Christ.
- Pentecost: The celebration of the Holy Spirit being poured out on the church.

ADVENT

CALL TO WORSHIP

Jeremiah 33:14–16
Behold, the days are coming, declares the LORD, when I will fulfill the promise I made to the house of Israel and the house of Judah. In those days and at that time I will cause a righteous Branch to spring up for David, and he shall execute justice and righteousness in the land. In those days Judah will be saved, and Jerusalem will dwell securely. And this is the name by which it will be called: "The LORD is our righteousness."

VOTUM

Psalm 124:8
Our help is in the name of the LORD, who made heaven and earth.

CONFESSION

Almighty God, give us grace that we may cast away the works of darkness, and put upon us the armour of light, now in the time of this mortal life, in which thy Son Jesus Christ came to visit us in great humility; that in the last day, when he shall come again in his glorious majesty to judge both the quick and the dead, we may rise to the life immortal, through him who liveth and reigneth with thee and the Holy Ghost, now and ever. Amen. (*The Book of Common Prayer*, 1892)

ASSURANCE OF FORGIVENESS

1 Timothy 1:15
The saying is trustworthy and deserving of full acceptance, that
Christ Jesus came into the world to save sinners, of whom I am
the foremost.

PSALM OF PRAISE

Psalm 85
LORD, you were favorable to your land;
    you restored the fortunes of Jacob.
You forgave the iniquity of your people;
    you covered all their sin. *Selah*
You withdrew all your wrath;
    you turned from your hot anger.
Restore us again, O God of our salvation,
    and put away your indignation toward us!
Will you be angry with us forever?
    Will you prolong your anger to all generations?
Will you not revive us again,
    that your people may rejoice in you?
Show us your steadfast love, O LORD,
    and grant us your salvation.
Let me hear what God the LORD will speak,
    for he will speak peace to his people, to his saints;
    but let them not turn back to folly.
Surely his salvation is near to those who fear him,
    that glory may dwell in our land.

Steadfast love and faithfulness meet;
  righteousness and peace kiss each other.
Faithfulness springs up from the ground,
  and righteousness looks down from the sky.
Yes, the LORD will give what is good,
  and our land will yield its increase.
Righteousness will go before him
  and make his footsteps a way.

PRAYER OF ILLUMINATION

Herein is wisdom; when I was undone, with no will to return to him, and no intellect to devise recovery, he came, God-incarnate, to save me to the uttermost, as man to die my death, to shed satisfying blood on my behalf, to work out a perfect righteousness for me! O God, take me in spirit to the watchful shepherds, and enlarge my mind! (*The Valley of Vision*[50])

DAILY BIBLE READING

Use the Bible Reading Plan of your choice.

DAILY INTERCESSION

Pray for:

>   Missions and Evangelism
>   Local church members and needs
>   Global, National and Local Leaders and Issues
>   Personal Needs and Holiness

THE LORD'S PRAYER

Our Father in heaven, hallowed be Your name, Your kingdom come, Your will be done, on earth as in heaven. Give us today our daily bread. Forgive us our sins, as we forgive those who sin against us. Lead us not into temptation, but deliver us from evil. For the kingdom, the power, and the glory are Yours now and forever. Amen.

DOXOLOGY

Sing or say these words out loud:

> Praise God from whom all blessings flow;
> Praise Him all creatures here below;
> Praise Him above ye heavenly hosts;
> Praise Father, Son and Holy Ghost.
> Amen.

CHRISTMAS

CALL TO WORSHIP

Luke 1:67–69

And his father Zechariah was filled with the Holy Spirit and prophesied, saying, "Blessed be the Lord God of Israel, for he has visited and redeemed his people and has raised up a horn of salvation for us in the house of his servant David."

VOTUM

Psalm 124:8

Our help is in the name of the LORD, who made heaven and earth.

CONFESSION

I, poor sinner, confess myself before God Almighty, that I have gravely sinned by the transgression of his commandments; that I have done many things which I should have left undone, and i have left undone that which I should have done, through unbelief and distrust in God and weakness of love toward my fellow servants. God knows the guilt that I have incurred, for which I am grieved. Be gracious to me, Lord. Be merciful to me, a poor sinner. Amen. (Diebold Schwarz[51])

ASSURANCE OF FORGIVENESS

1 John 5:1
Everyone who believes that Jesus is the Christ has been born of
God, and everyone who loves the Father loves whoever has been
born of him.

PSALM OF PRAISE

Psalm 97
The LORD reigns, let the earth rejoice;
    let the many coastlands be glad!
Clouds and thick darkness are all around him;
    righteousness and justice are the foundation of his throne.
Fire goes before him
    and burns up his adversaries all around.
His lightnings light up the world;
    the earth sees and trembles.
The mountains melt like wax before the LORD,
    before the Lord of all the earth.
The heavens proclaim his righteousness,
    and all the peoples see his glory.
All worshipers of images are put to shame,
    who make their boast in worthless idols;
    worship him, all you gods!
Zion hears and is glad,
    and the daughters of Judah rejoice,
    because of your judgments, O LORD.
For you, O LORD, are most high over all the earth;
    you are exalted far above all gods.

O you who love the LORD, hate evil!
    He preserves the lives of his saints;
    he delivers them from the hand of the wicked.
Light is sown for the righteous,
    and joy for the upright in heart.
Rejoice in the LORD, O you righteous,
    and give thanks to his holy name!

PRAYER OF ILLUMINATION

Almighty and eternal God, we humbly pray, grant that we may know and praise your dear Son as holy Simeon did, who took him up in his arms, spiritually knew and confessed him; through the same, Jesus Christ our Lord. Amen. (Martin Luther[52])

DAILY BIBLE READING

Use the Bible Reading Plan of your choice.

DAILY INTERCESSION

Pray for:

    Missions and Evangelism
    Local church members and needs
    Global, National and Local Leaders and Issues
    Personal Needs and Holiness

THE LORD'S PRAYER

Our Father in heaven, hallowed be Your name, Your kingdom come, Your will be done, on earth as in heaven. Give us today our daily bread. Forgive us our sins, as we forgive those who sin against us. Lead us not into temptation, but deliver us from evil. For the kingdom, the power, and the glory are Yours now and forever. Amen.

DOXOLOGY

Sing or say these words out loud:

> Praise God from whom all blessings flow;
> Praise Him all creatures here below;
> Praise Him above ye heavenly hosts;
> Praise Father, Son and Holy Ghost.
> Amen.

Epiphany

CALL TO WORSHIP

Matthew 2:9–11

After listening to the king, they went on their way. And behold, the star that they had seen when it rose went before them until it came to rest over the place where the child was. When they saw the star, they rejoiced exceedingly with great joy. And going into the house, they saw the child with Mary his mother, and they fell down and worshiped him. Then, opening their treasures, they offered him gifts, gold and frankincense and myrrh.

VOTUM

Psalm 124:8

Our help is in the name of the LORD, who made heaven and earth.

CONFESSION

Lord Jesus, our great high priest, surely you are faithful. Surely you will do the work of the high priest for my soul. I have sinned, and sinned greatly. But Lord, it is the work of our high priest to clear my debt. Now, Lord Jesus, I come to you as my high priest. Resolve this for me. I confess that my own conscience accuses me. Satan accuses me. Moses accuses me. But it is the work of our great high priest to remove all accusations brought against poor believers. So now Lord, I do come to you as my great high priest. Take away the accusations. When I look at what I do, there is so much deadness, so much hardness of heart, and so many distractions. I am afraid my best will never be enough. But Lord, it is the job of our great high priest to take away the weeds of the work we do, and to present it to God. Now, O Lord, I come to you as my great high priest. Carry my prayers to God the Father. Amen. (William Bridge[53])

ASSURANCE OF FORGIVENESS

Ephesians 2:12-16
Remember that you were at that time separated from Christ, alienated from the commonwealth of Israel and strangers to the covenants of promise, having no hope and without God in the world. But now in Christ Jesus you who once were far off have been brought near by the blood of Christ. For he himself is our peace, who has made us both one and has broken down in his flesh the dividing wall of hostility by abolishing the law of commandments expressed in ordinances, that he might create in himself one new man in place of the two, so making peace, and might reconcile us both to God in one body through the cross, thereby killing the hostility.

PSALM OF PRAISE

Psalm 67
May God be gracious to us and bless us
    and make his face to shine upon us, *Selah*
that your way may be known on earth,
    your saving power among all nations.

Let the peoples praise you, O God;
  let all the peoples praise you!
Let the nations be glad and sing for joy,
    for you judge the peoples with equity
    and guide the nations upon earth. *Selah*
Let the peoples praise you, O God;
  let all the peoples praise you!
The earth has yielded its increase;
  God, our God, shall bless us.
God shall bless us;
  let all the ends of the earth fear him!

PRAYER OF ILLUMINATION

O Lord, we beseech thee mercifully to receive the prayers of thy people who call upon thee; and grant that they may both perceive and know what things they ought to do, and also may have grace and power faithfully to fulfill the same; through Jesus Christ our Lord. Amen. (*The Book of Common Prayer*, 1892)

DAILY BIBLE READING

Use the Bible Reading Plan of your choice.

DAILY INTERCESSION

Pray for:

    Missions and Evangelism
    Local church members and needs

Global, National and Local Leaders and Issues
Personal Needs and Holiness

THE LORD'S PRAYER

Our Father in heaven, hallowed be Your name, Your kingdom come, Your will be done, on earth as in heaven. Give us today our daily bread. Forgive us our sins, as we forgive those who sin against us. Lead us not into temptation, but deliver us from evil. For the kingdom, the power, and the glory are Yours now and forever. Amen.

DOXOLOGY

Sing or say these words out loud:

> Praise God from whom all blessings flow;
> Praise Him all creatures here below;
> Praise Him above ye heavenly hosts;
> Praise Father, Son and Holy Ghost.
> Amen.

Good Friday

CALL TO WORSHIP

Jude 24–25

Now to him who is able to keep you from stumbling and to present you blameless before the presence of his glory with great joy, to the only God, our Savior, through Jesus Christ our Lord, be glory, majesty, dominion, and authority, before all time and now and forever. Amen.

VOTUM

Psalm 124:8

Our help is in the name of the LORD, who made heaven and earth.

CONFESSION

Lord, I caused your sorrows. My sin brought about your shame, my failings your injuries. I committed the fault, and you are plagued for the offense. I am guilty, and you are charged. I sinned, and you suffered the death. You hung on the cross. Oh the deepness of God's love, the wonder of his grace! Mercy without measure! What can I say? I was proud; you are humble. I was disobedient; you became obedient. I are the forbidden fruit; you hung on the cursed tree. O Lord, let me never forget your infinite love. Amen. (Lewis Bayly[54])

ASSURANCE OF FORGIVENESS

1 Peter 2:24
He himself bore our sins in his body on the tree, that we might die to sin and live to righteousness. By his wounds you have been healed.

PSALM OF PRAISE

Psalm 2
Why do the nations rage
    and the peoples plot in vain?
The kings of the earth set themselves,
    and the rulers take counsel together,
    against the LORD and against his Anointed, saying,
"Let us burst their bonds apart
    and cast away their cords from us."
He who sits in the heavens laughs;
    the Lord holds them in derision.
Then he will speak to them in his wrath,
    and terrify them in his fury, saying,
"As for me, I have set my King
    on Zion, my holy hill."
I will tell of the decree:
The LORD said to me, "You are my Son;
    today I have begotten you.
Ask of me, and I will make the nations your heritage,
    and the ends of the earth your possession.
You shall break them with a rod of iron
    and dash them in pieces like a potter's vessel."

Now therefore, O kings, be wise;
    be warned, O rulers of the earth.
Serve the LORD with fear,
    and rejoice with trembling.
Kiss the Son,
    lest he be angry, and you perish in the way,
    for his wrath is quickly kindled.
Blessed are all who take refuge in him.

PRAYER OF ILLUMINATION

O blessed hand of Jesus, drive in the nail of divine love! Smite hard, Lord. Force out the rusted iron of my selfishness. Let not a fragment of it remain. Love alone can vanquish love. Thyself alone can conquer self in me. No secondary force will suffice. My God, thou must display thy Godhead's power of love, or my vile heart will never part with self. Amen. (Charles Spurgeon[55])

DAILY BIBLE READING

Use the Bible Reading Plan of your choice.

DAILY INTERCESSION

Pray for:

    Missions and Evangelism
    Local church members and needs
    Global, National and Local Leaders and Issues
    Personal Needs and Holiness

THE LORD'S PRAYER

Our Father in heaven, hallowed be Your name, Your kingdom come, Your will be done, on earth as in heaven. Give us today our daily bread. Forgive us our sins, as we forgive those who sin against us. Lead us not into temptation, but deliver us from evil. For the kingdom, the power, and the glory are Yours now and forever. Amen.

DOXOLOGY

Sing or say these words out loud:

> Praise God from whom all blessings flow;
> Praise Him all creatures here below;
> Praise Him above ye heavenly hosts;
> Praise Father, Son and Holy Ghost.
> Amen.

Easter

CALL TO WORSHIP

1 Corinthians 15:55–57
O death, where is your victory? O death, where is your sting? The sting of death is sin, and the power of sin is the law. But thanks be to God, who gives us the victory through our Lord Jesus Christ.

VOTUM

Psalm 124:8
Our help is in the name of the LORD, who made heaven and earth.

CONFESSION

O eternal God and most merciful Father, we confess and acknowledge here, before your Divine Majesty, that we are miserable sinners, conceived and born in sin and iniquity, so that in us there is no goodness. For the flesh evermore rebels against the spirit, whereby we continually transgress your holy precepts and commandments, and so purchase to ourselves, through your just judgment, death and damnation. Nevertheless, heavenly Father, since we are displeased with ourselves for the sins that we have committed against you, and sincerely repent of the same, we most humbly ask you, for Jesus Christ's sake, to show mercy upon us, to forgive us all our sins, and to increase your Holy Spirit in us. (John Knox[56])

ASSURANCE OF FORGIVENESS

Romans 8:11
If the Spirit of him who raised Jesus from the dead dwells in you,
he who raised Christ Jesus from the dead will also give life to your
mortal bodies through his Spirit who dwells in you.

PSALM OF PRAISE

Psalm 28
To you, O LORD, I call;
  my rock, be not deaf to me,
lest, if you be silent to me,
  I become like those who go down to the pit.
Hear the voice of my pleas for mercy,
  when I cry to you for help,
when I lift up my hands
  toward your most holy sanctuary.
Do not drag me off with the wicked,
  with the workers of evil,
who speak peace with their neighbors
  while evil is in their hearts.
Give to them according to their work
  and according to the evil of their deeds;
give to them according to the work of their hands;
  render them their due reward.
Because they do not regard the works of the LORD
  or the work of his hands,
he will tear them down and build them up no more.

Blessed be the LORD!
  For he has heard the voice of my pleas for mercy.
The LORD is my strength and my shield;
  in him my heart trusts, and I am helped;
my heart exults,
  and with my song I give thanks to him.
The LORD is the strength of his people;
  he is the saving refuge of his anointed.
Oh, save your people and bless your heritage!
  Be their shepherd and carry them forever.

PRAYER OF ILLUMINATION

Almighty God, who through thine only-begotten Son Jesus Christ hast overcome death, and opened unto us the gate of everlasting life; We humbly beseech thee that, as by thy special grace preventing us thou dost put into our minds good desires, so by thy continual help we may bring the same to good effect; through* Jesus Christ our Lord, who liveth and reigneth with thee and the Holy Ghost ever, one God, world without end. Amen. (*The Book of Common Prayer*, 1892)

DAILY BIBLE READING

Use the Bible Reading Plan of your choice.

DAILY INTERCESSION

Pray for:

Missions and Evangelism
Local church members and needs
Global, National and Local Leaders and Issues
Personal Needs and Holiness

THE LORD'S PRAYER

Our Father in heaven, hallowed be Your name, Your kingdom
come, Your will be done, on earth as in heaven. Give us today
our daily bread. Forgive us our sins, as we forgive those who sin
against us. Lead us not into temptation, but deliver us from evil.
For the kingdom, the power, and the glory are Yours now and
forever. Amen.

DOXOLOGY

Sing or say these words out loud:

Praise God from whom all blessings flow;
Praise Him all creatures here below;
Praise Him above ye heavenly hosts;
Praise Father, Son and Holy Ghost.
Amen.

Pentecost

CALL TO WORSHIP

Ezekiel 37:14
And I will put my Spirit within you, and you shall live, and I will place you in your own land. Then you shall know that I am the LORD; I have spoken, and I will do it, declares the LORD."

VOTUM

Psalm 124:8
Our help is in the name of the LORD, who made heaven and earth.

CONFESSION

Alas, O Father, that is true, we acknowledge our sin and trespass. Yet be Thou a merciful father, and deal not with us according to our deservings, neither judge us by the rigorousness of Thy will, but give us grace that we may so live that Thy holy name may be hallowed and sanctified in us. And keep our hearts, that we neither do nor speak, no, that we not once think or purpose anything but that which is to Thy honor and praise, and above all things make Thy name and honor to be sought of us and not our own name and vain glory. And of Thy mighty power bring to pass in us that we may love and fear Thee as a son his father. Amen. (William Tyndale[57])

ASSURANCE OF FORGIVENESS

Acts 2:17–21

And in the last days it shall be, God declares, that I will pour out my Spirit on all flesh, and your sons and your daughters shall prophesy, and your young men shall see visions, and your old men shall dream dreams; even on my male servants and female servants in those days I will pour out my Spirit, and they shall prophesy. And I will show wonders in the heavens above and signs on the earth below, blood, and fire, and vapor of smoke; the sun shall be turned to darkness and the moon to blood, before the day of the Lord comes, the great and magnificent day. And it shall come to pass that everyone who calls upon the name of the Lord shall be saved.

PSALM OF PRAISE

Psalm 121

I lift up my eyes to the hills.
　　From where does my help come?
My help comes from the LORD,
　　who made heaven and earth.
He will not let your foot be moved;
　　he who keeps you will not slumber.
Behold, he who keeps Israel
　　will neither slumber nor sleep.
The LORD is your keeper;
　　the LORD is your shade on your right hand.
The sun shall not strike you by day,
　　nor the moon by night.

The LORD will keep you from all evil;
>   he will keep your life.
The LORD will keep
>   your going out and your coming in
>   from this time forth and forevermore.

PRAYER OF ILLUMINATION

O God, who as at this time didst teach the hearts of thy faithful people, by sending* to them the light of thy Holy Spirit; Grant us by the same Spirit to have a right judgment in all things, and evermore to rejoice in his holy comfort; through the merits of Christ Jesus our Saviour, who liveth and reigneth with thee, in the unity of the same Spirit, one God, world without end. Amen. (*The Book of Common Prayer* 1789)

DAILY BIBLE READING

Use the Bible Reading Plan of your choice.

DAILY INTERCESSION

Pray for:

>   Missions and Evangelism
>   Local church members and needs
>   Global, National and Local Leaders and Issues
>   Personal Needs and Holiness

THE LORD'S PRAYER

Our Father in heaven, hallowed be Your name, Your kingdom come, Your will be done, on earth as in heaven. Give us today our daily bread. Forgive us our sins, as we forgive those who sin against us. Lead us not into temptation, but deliver us from evil. For the kingdom, the power, and the glory are Yours now and forever. Amen.

DOXOLOGY

Sing or say these words out loud:

> Praise God from whom all blessings flow;
> Praise Him all creatures here below;
> Praise Him above ye heavenly hosts;
> Praise Father, Son and Holy Ghost.
> Amen.

Sources

[1] "A Prayer for Revival." Philip Doddridge. *Piercing Heaven: Prayers of the Puritans*, edited by Robert Elmer, Lexham Press, 2012, 77–79.

[2] Zwingli, Ulrich. "Ulrich Zwingli's Prayer." *Jaquelle Crowe*, 10 Oct. 2012, https://www.jaquellecrowe.com/blog/2012/10/ulrich-zwinglis-prayer.html.

[3] Gibson, Jonathan. *Reformation Worship: Liturgies from the Past for the Present*. New Growth Press, 2018, 287.

[4] Wesley, John. "Prayer of Confession: John Wesley." *Artistic Theologian*, 12 April 2018, https://artistictheologian.com/2018/04/12/prayer-of-confession-john-wesley/.

[5] *The Baptist Confession of Faith* (1689), 1:6.

[6] Augustine. *Confessions*. Baker Book House, 2005, 21.

[7] "Make My Heart the Good Ground." Lewis Bayly. *Piercing Heaven: Prayers of the Puritans*, edited by Robert Elmer, Lexham Press, 2012, 165.

[8] Spurgeon, *Charles Haddon. The Pastor in Prayer*. Banner of Truth Trust, 2017, 16.

9 Gibson, Jonathan. *Reformation Worship: Liturgies from the Past for the Present.* New Growth Press, 2018, 323.

10 Luther, Martin. "The Empty Vessel." *A Collection of Prayers,* https://acollectionofprayers.com/2016/06/20/the-empty-vessel/.

11 "To the Holy Spirit." Richard Baxter. *Piercing Heaven: Prayers of the Puritans,* edited by Robert Elmer, Lexham Press, 2012, 270.

12 "Before a Sermon." Edward Reynolds. *Piercing Heaven: Prayers of the Puritans,* edited by Robert Elmer, Lexham Press, 2012, 138.

13 "In Humility." Robert Hawker. *Piercing Heaven: Prayers of the Puritans,* edited by Robert Elmer, Lexham Press, 2012, 199.

14 Gibson, Jonathan. *Reformation Worship: Liturgies from the Past for the Present.* New Growth Press, 2018, 650.

15 Chester, Tim. *Into His Presence: Praying with the Puritans.* The Good Book Company, 2022, 65.

16 Thomas A Kempis. "A Collection of Prayers." Edited by Paul C. Stratman, https://acollectionofprayers.com/tag/thomas-a-kempis/.

17 Ambrose. "Early Christian Prayers." *Faith and Worship,* https://www.faithandworship.com/early_Christian_prayers.htm#gsc.tab=0.

[18] Gibson, Jonathan. *Reformation Worship: Liturgies from the Past for the Present.* New Growth Press, 2018, 222.

[19] Durer, Albrecht. "A Prayer for the Safety of Martin Luther." *The Art History Project*, n.d., https://www.arthistoryproject.com/artists/albrecht-durer/a-prayer-for-the-safety-of-martin-luther/.

[20] Luther, Martin. "Help Us to Know Your Word, Help Us to Do Our Work." *A Collection of Prayers*, https://acollectionofprayers.com/2017/06/26/help-us-to-know-your-word-help-us-to-do-our-work/.

[21] "Grace for the Weary." William Bridge. *Piercing Heaven: Prayers of the Puritans*, edited by Robert Elmer, Lexham Press, 2012, 28.

[22] Herbert, George. "The Holy Scriptures." *The Temple.* Christian Classics Ethereal Library, https://ccel.org/ccel/herbert/temple2/temple2.xli.html#:~:text=O%20make%20thy%20word%20a,for%20which%20it%20is%20given.

[23] "Come, Holy Spirit." Robert Hawker. *Piercing Heaven: Prayers of the Puritans*, edited by Robert Elmer, Lexham Press, 2012, 47.

[24] Gibson, Jonathan. *Reformation Worship: Liturgies from the Past for the Present.* New Growth Press, 2018, 649–650.

[25] Spurgeon, Charles Haddon. *The Pastor in Prayer.* Banner of Truth Trust, 2017, 18.

26 Durer, Albrecht. "Help Us Recognize Your Voice." *A Collection of Prayers*, 23 June 2016, https://acollectionofprayers.com/2016/06/23/help-us-recognize-your-voice/.

27 Owen, John. "The Death of Death in the Death of Christ." Christian Classics Ethereal Library, https://ccel.org/ccel/owen/mort/mort.i.xvii.html.

28 Luther, Martin. "Let Your Word Shine." *Just Prayer*, GraceSpace, https://www.justprayer.gracespace.info/let-your-word-shine-martin-luther/.

29 Spurgeon, Charles Haddon. *The Pastor in Prayer*. Banner of Truth Trust, 2017, 18.

30 "No One Speaks Like Jesus." Robert Hawker. *Piercing Heaven: Prayers of the Puritans*, edited by Robert Elmer, Lexham Press, 2012, 48.

31 "The Belgic Confession (Circa 1561 A.D.)." *A Puritan's Mind*, https://www.apuritansmind.com/creeds-and-confessions/the-belgic-confession-circa-1561-a-d/.

32 Luther, Martin. "Only For Your Glory." *A Collection of Prayers*, https://acollectionofprayers.com/tag/martin-luther/page/3/.

33 Winslow, Octavious. "What Lord! After All I Have Done!" *Grace Gems*, https://www.gracegems.org/03/done.html.

[34] "Open Our Eyes, Lord." William Ames. *Piercing Heaven: Prayers of the Puritans*, edited by Robert Elmer, Lexham Press, 2012, 111.

[35] "Prayer of a Convicted Sinner." Phillip Doddridge. *Piercing Heaven: Prayers of the Puritans*, edited by Robert Elmer, Lexham Press, 2012, 204.

[36] Augustine. *Confessions*. Baker Book House, 2005, 20.

[37] "A Cry for Redeeming Grace." David Clarkson. *Piercing Heaven: Prayers of the Puritans*, edited by Robert Elmer, Lexham Press, 2012, 20.

[38] Henry, Matthew. *The Quest for Meekness and the Quietness of Spirit*. Wipf and Stock Publishers, 2007, 19.

[39] Cranmer, Thomas. "Shine in Our Hearts" *A Collection of Prayers*, https://acollectionofprayers.com/tag/thomas-cranmer/.

[40] Dietrich, Veit. "Sexagesima Sunday," Veit Dietrich *Collects*. Translated by Paul C. Stratman, 2016, https://acollectionofprayers.files.wordpress.com/2016/08/veit-dietrich-collects-ce3.pdf.

[41] Sibbes, Richard. *The Bruised Reed*. Revised ed., Banner of Truth, 1998, 138.

[42] "Spiritual Growth." *The Valley of Vision: A Collection of Puritan Prayers and Devotions*. Edited by Arthur Bennett, Banner of Truth Trust, 2002, 201.

[43] Baxter, Richard. *Dying Thoughts*. Banner of Truth Trust, 2004, 89–90.

[44] Luther, Martin. "Prayers When Reading the Word." *A Collection of Prayers*, https://acollectionofprayers.com/tag/martin-luther/page/3/

[45] Watson, Thomas. *The Doctrine of Repentance*. Banner of Truth Trust, 1987, 35.

[46] "Is My Name Written on God's Heart?" Isaac Ambrose. *Piercing Heaven: Prayers of the Puritans*, edited by Robert Elmer, Lexham Press, 2012, 25.

[47] "Give Us a Nobler Mind." Phillip Doddridge. *Piercing Heaven: Prayers of the Puritans*, edited by Robert Elmer, Lexham Press, 2012, 42.

[48] Knox, John. "The Third Book of Discipline: Of Prayers," Christian Classics Ethereal Library, https://ccel.org/ccel/knox/prayer/prayer.iii.html.

[49] "Before a Sermon." Edward Reynolds. *Piercing Heaven: Prayers of the Puritans*, edited by Robert Elmer, Lexham Press, 2012, 138.

[50] "Spiritual Growth." *The Valley of Vision: A Collection of Puritan Prayers and Devotions*. Edited by Arthur Bennett, Banner of Truth Trust, 2002, 28–29.

[51] Gibson, Jonathan. *Reformation Worship: Liturgies from the Past for the Present*. New Growth Press, 2018, 167.

[52] Luther, Martin. "Nunc Dimmitis and Prayer," Collection of Prayers, https://acollectionofprayers.com/tag/martin-luther/page/2/.

[53] "Coming to the High Priest." William Bridge. *Piercing Heaven: Prayers of the Puritans*, edited by Robert Elmer, Lexham Press, 2012, 27.

[54] "I Am the One to Blame." Lewis Bayly. *Piercing Heaven: Prayers of the Puritans*, edited by Robert Elmer, Lexham Press, 2012, 202–203.

[55] Spurgeon, Charles. *Flowers from a Puritan's Garden*. Banner of Truth Trust, 2017, 103.

[56] Gibson, Jonathan. *Reformation Worship: Liturgies from the Past for the Present*. New Growth Press, 2018, 569–570.

[57] Tyndale, William. "William Tyndale's Prayers." S-Life, 2021, https://slife.org/william-tyndales-prayers/.

Made in the USA
Columbia, SC
12 December 2024

49148894R00093